Springer Series in Language and Communication 4

Editor: W. J. M. Levelt

Springer Series in Language and Communication

Editor: W. J. M. Levelt

Leonard G. M. Noordman

Inferring
from Language

With a Foreword by Herbert H. Clark

With 4 Figures

Springer-Verlag Berlin Heidelberg New York 1979

Dr. Leonard G. M. Noordman

Department of Psychology, University of Groningen
The Netherlands

Temporary address:

Department of Psychology, Carnegie-Mellon University
Pittsburgh, PA 15213, USA

Series Editor:

Professor Dr. Willem J. M. Levelt

Max-Planck-Gesellschaft zur Förderung der Wissenschaften e.V.
Projektgruppe für Psycholinguistik
Berg en Dalseweg 79, Nijmegen, The Netherlands

BC
57
.N66

ISBN 3-540-09386-9 Springer-Verlag Berlin Heidelberg New York
ISBN 0-387-09386-9 Springer-Verlag New York Heidelberg Berlin

Library of Congress Cataloging in Publication Data Noordman, Leonard G.M. 1940-. Inferring from language.
(Springer series in language and communication; v. 4) Includes bibliographical references and indexes. 1.
Language and logic. 2. Inference (Logic). 3. Reasoning. 4. Ordinary-language philosophy. I. Title. II. Series.
BC57.N66   153   79-12190

The use of registered names, trademarks, etc. in this publication does not imply, even in the absence of a specific
statement, that such names are exempt from the relevant protective laws and regulations and therefore free for
general use.

Offset printing and bookbinding: Brühlsche Universitätsdruckerei, Lahn-Giessen
2153/3130-543210

Foreword

In the study of human thought there could hardly be a more fundamental concern than language and reasoning. In the tradition of Western philosophy, humans are distinguished by their ability to speak and to think rationally. And language is often considered a prerequisite for rational thought. If psychologists, then, are ever to discover what is truly human about their species, they will have to discover how language is produced and understood, and how it plays a role in reasoning and other forms of rational thought.

Within psychology there has been an imperative to study language and reasoning together. Since Wundt, psychologists have succeeded in building a theoretical foundation for both language and reasoning. What has become clear from these beginnings is that the two are inextricably bound to each other. Like the two players in a chess game, take away one of them and the game no longer exists. On the one hand, producing and understanding speech requires an intricate process of reasoning. Speakers must rationally choose sentences that will affect their listeners in ways they intend, and listeners must infer what speakers could conceivably have meant in selecting the sentences they did. Reasoning, inference, and rational thought lie at the very center of speaking and listening. On the other hand, logical reasoning begins with, and is influenced by, the language in which a problem is stated. The classical Aristotelian syllogism - *All men are mortal; Socrates is a man; therefore, Socrates is mortal* - is reasoned out as much on the basis of what words like *all, man, is,* and *mortal* mean as on the basis of any independent process of reasoning.

In this monograph Dr. Noordman has studied this chessboard of language and reasoning and has turned up some remarkable findings. Not only has he discovered new facts about language and reasoning separately, but he has also been able to demonstrate how they interact in complicated but predictable ways.

In the first part of the monograph Dr. Noordman takes up one of the most widely used types of syllogism within psychology - the three-term series problem. Example: *John is bigger than Pete; Bill is smaller than Pete; who is*

smallest? Since Burt's and Piaget's work with this problem about 50 years
ago, it has been known that solving these problems is profoundly affected
by the language in which they are stated. What Dr. Noordman has done is lay
bare a number of sources of these influences and suggest how they play a
role in the process by which the answers are arrived at. This study provides
an example par excellence of how language influences reasoning and how reasoning works on the basis of language.

In the second part of this monograph, Dr. Noordman considers a much purer
form of inference - the understanding of conditional sentences. This amounts
to an investigation of how *if* and its logical cousins are understood in various circumstances. *If*, of course, is an ordinary subordinate conjunction
and so, one might ask, what is so complicated about it? But as Dr. Noordman
demonstrates, *if* is a linguistic chameleon. It changes meaning from one context to the next, and while it is easy to see and grasp in one context, it
is very difficult to grasp in another. Happily, these changes appear to be
systematic and thus open to investigation. Yet the chameleonlike quality of
if surely complicates our view of reasoning. Since the beginning of modern
philosophical logic, *if* has been at the center of the enterprise. If in ordinary language *if* does not have the constancy that it has been stipulated
to have in logic, then it may be impossible to translate models of philosophical logic directly into models of human reasoning. Without understanding *if*
in natural language, therefore, there is little chance we will ever properly
understand reasoning and inference as it is done by humans. Dr. Noordman's
investigations take us a long way toward that goal.

In the third and final part of the monograph, Dr. Noordman has broken
away from well-known problems to show us quite a new linguistic factor in
reasoning - the distinction between foregrounded and backgrounded information.
Imagine that a friend says to us, "My neighbor isn't a bachelor". From this
we would ordinarily infer that the neighbor was a married man, not that the
neighbor was an unmarried woman. In Noordman's terminology, for *bachelor* the
attribute of being unmarried is foregrounded information and is therefore
readily susceptible to negation, while the attribute of being male is backgrounded information and is not so susceptible to negation. So far, this
seems to be a nice linguistic distinction, but what could it possibly have
to do with reasoning? As Dr. Noordman demonstrates, it has dramatic consequences for inferences people are willing to draw and the speed with which
they are willing to draw them. It may well be, in fact, that foregrounded
and backgrounded information are among the most important influences on reasoning yet investigated.

Whenever psychologists tackle such issues as the relation between language and reasoning, the real challenge is to devise tools sharp enough to dissect the issues neatly and easily. When the issue is a new one, like the influence of foregrounded and backgrounded information on reasoning, the challenge is especially great since there are generally no tools readily available and the psychologist has to fall back in his own ingenuity. In the third part of this monograph we see an excellent example of how this challenge is sometimes met in most unexpected ways. There is a well-known riddle that goes as follows: "Two Indians, a tall one and a short one, were sitting on a fence; the shorter one was the son of the taller one; the taller one was not the father of the shorter one. How is that possible?" This riddle is not easy for most people to solve, but for most of us it is otherwise just an intellectual curiosity. It took Dr. Noordman to see its potential as a tool for studying foregrounded and backgrounded information, and indeed the tool has served him well. As the third part of this monograph reveals, it has led to provocative new findings about the role of foregrounded and background information in inference.

Like all other monographs worthy of our attention, this monograph raises new questions in the very act of answering old ones. It shows us how far we have yet to go for a complete understanding of language and reasoning. This is no surprise. Yet this monograph leaves us with a great deal of optimism. It reaffirms our conviction that we are making genuine progress toward the understanding of human thought.

Stanford University   Herbert H. Clark
May, 1979

Acknowledgments

I am greatly indebted to the series editor Dr. W.J.M. Levelt for his continued encouragement, discussions, helpful suggestions, and for his comments on the manuscript. Thanks are also due to Dr. J.A. Michon who has read and commented on the whole manuscript. I wish to thank the staff of the Institute for Experimental Psychology of Groningen University for the construction of the equipment, many students and research assistants for their help in conducting experiments, and Ms. E. Maarschalkerweerd for typing carefully the manuscript.

This research was supported in part by a grant from the Netherlands Organization for the Advancement of Pure Research (Z.W.O.) to the author and to Dr. W. Noordman-Vonk and at an earlier stage by a grant from the Niels Stensen Stichting.

Leonard G.M. Noordman

Contents

XII

Chapter 1   Introduction

1.1 Cognition and Language Behavior

The present study is concerned with verbal behavior considered from a cognitive point of view. The verbal behaviors that are studied are central cognitive processes such as comprehension, inferring, and reasoning. The tasks
that are studied require subjects to integrate pieces of incoming information with each other as well as with stored knowledge and to draw inferences
on the basis of the processed information. It is clear that comprehension of
the information is at the heart of these tasks. Because comprehension is
assumed to include inferential processes, the comprehension tasks can as
well be called reasoning tasks or inference tasks.

Language material constitutes the basis for the experimental subject's
understanding and inferences. This behavior in its turn constitutes the basis for the psychologist's inferring from language. Language understanding
and inferring from language are studied because they may provide insight
into human cognitive functioning. This is borne out by the history of experimental work on comprehension. The integration of information in the comprehension process has been studied as early as the origin of experimental
psychology. The works of Wundt, Binet and Henri, Henderson, Peterson, Arnold
and Bühler, discussed in BLUMENTHAL (1974) resemble recent work in cognition, especially as far as the processing of semantic information in comprehension is concerned.

The interest in language for the study of human cognition is apparent in
two other disciplines that have a great impact on cognitive psychology: linguistics and artificial intelligence. The impact is such that in many cases
the distinction between the different disciplines becomes less and less obvious. According to CHOMSKY (1968): "a linguist (...) is attempting to characterize knowledge of a language, a certain cognitive system that has been
developed (...) by the normal speaker-hearer... [The linguist] is trying to
establish certain general properties of human intelligence. Linguistics, so
characterized, is simply the subfield of psychology that deals with these

aspects of mind" (p. 24). The same concern with cognition is manifest in the field of artificial intelligence: BOBROW and COLLINS (1975) define the discipline of cognitive science "as a new field containing elements from psychology, linguistics, computer science, philosophy, education and artificial intelligence" (p. 2).

The generally recognized importance of research on language for the understanding of central cognitive processes is the motivation for the present research, but no attempt will be made to discuss this relation in detail. Language behavior will be investigated as a form of cognition.

1.2 Comprehension and Inferences

The present study consists of three rather independent series of experiments on comprehension and inferential processes. A short characterization of the notion of comprehension will be given first.

The common core in the various views of sentence comprehension can be described as the integration of incoming (new) information with existing (old) information. This core notion can be illustrated by a few quotations from quite diverse authors. According to KINTSCH (1977) "comprehension involves integrating information from different sentences, organizing and supplementing it through inferences from what one already knows, rather than merely interpreting what is directly expressed by a sentence" (p. 332). HAVILAND and CLARK (1974) claim that the words "understanding" or "comprehension" "refer to the way we take in the meaning of a sentence and integrate it with information we already know - from context and from past memory" (p. 512). According to CARPENTER and JUST (1976) "sentence comprehension consists of extracting the relevant information from a sentence and, when possible, integrating that information with other semantic or procedural knowledge" (p. 318). CARROLL (1972) considers comprehension "as a process that contains at least two stages: (a) apprehension of linguistic information, and (b) relating that information to wider context" (p.13). The second stage may require processes of inference, according to CARROLL.

Given this core notion of comprehension one might, however, find differences in the delimitation of the notion (see also CLARK, 1978). Investigators differ with respect to the range of contextual information that is subsumed in the definition of comprehension. At the one extreme, comprehension of a sentence is concerned with the derivation of the representation of the sentence, independent of its context. The comprehension process consists in deriving what linguists call the structural description of sentences. Such a view has been proposed by FODOR et al.(1974) and by TANENHAUS et al.(1976). This view is not adopted in the present study because of its narrowness. At the other extreme, comprehension is treated as a process that involves all kinds of world knowledge. All kinds of information that is prerequisite for comprehension, and inferences that are only indirectly related to the comprehension task, are subsumed under the notion of comprehension. This view is best illustrated by the work of BRANSFORD and JOHNSON (1973). CLARK (1978) proposes an intermediate position: "comprehension is conceived to be the process by which people arrive at the interpretation the speaker *intended* them to grasp for that utterance in that context (...) This view requires listeners to draw inferences that go well beyond the literal or direct meaning of a sentence."

The position adopted in the present study is that inference processes directly related to the task that subjects have to perform are considered as part of the comprehension process. According to this interpretation, inferring the intended meaning of a message should indeed be considered as an integral part of the comprehension process, as CLARK proposes.

1.3 Types of Comprehension Research

The process of sentence comprehension has been described in very general terms as the integration of new and old information. The new information is the information contained in the incoming sentences. Types of sentence-comprehension research can be differentiated according to the type of the old information with which the new information has to be integrated.

Sentence comprehension and perception. Comprehension of sentences with respect to nonlinguistic information has been studied extensively. These studies focussed on semantics and perception. Some examples are the works of CLARK and CHASE (1972); CLARK et al. (1973); OLSON and FILBY (1972); TRABASSO (1972); GLUCKSBERG et al. (1973). The aim of these studies is to develop an information processing model for the verification of sentences vis-à-vis pictures. These studies have arrived at detailed conclusions concerning the coding of sentences and the processes of matching sentences with pictures. An elegant and simple model that can account for much of this research has recently been proposed by CARPENTER and JUST (1975). An integration of experimental work on the perception of events, such as Michotte's classical mechanical motions, and a procedural semantics analysis of verbs of motion, has been proposed by LEVELT et al. (1978).

Sentence comprehension and knowledge of the world. The role of knowledge
of the world in comprehending sentences has been studied, e.g., by BRANSFORD
and FRANKS (1972) and by BRANSFORD and JOHNSON (1973). In the comprehension
process inferences are made based on knowledge of the world. Information
communicated by the sentences is integrated with knowledge of the world. In
this way the comprehension process is described as the construction of more
wholistic semantic representations. The comprehension process is described
very globally. No mechanisms are specified for the integration of old and
new information as is done in studies to be discussed shortly. The crucial
role of nonlinguistic information for the comprehension process is also
demonstrated by these studies in cases where the understanding fails. When
appropriate knowledge of the world is not available, e.g., in the case of a
story about an unknown knowledge domain, there is no old information with
respect to which the information in the sentences can be integrated. Comprehension and recall are greatly impaired in such cases. The integrative
aspect of comprehension has also been confirmed by FREDERIKSEN's research
(1975). He demonstrated that, during the acquisition of information, inferences and overgeneralizations are made which become an integral part of the
memory structure. The theory on the semantic integration of information, as
developed by BRANSFORD and FRANKS, has been challenged, however, by other
authors (REITMAN and BOWER, 1973; FLAGG, 1976).

Much work in the field of semantic memory may also be considered to deal
with comprehension as a process of matching information with stored knowledge. The emphasis in these studies is mainly on the verification of information. Research that has been done in this field has a high degree of
theoretical precision. References can be found in NOORDMAN-VONK (1979).

Sentence comprehension and other sentences. The comprehension of sentences with respect to other sentences has been studied, e.g., in experiments
on linear orderings (HUTTENLOCHER, 1968; CLARK, 1969a; POTTS, 1972) and in
verification experiments (ANDERSON, 1974; CARPENTER, 1973; GARROD and
TRABASSO, 1973; JUST and CLARK, 1973; STILLINGS, 1975), to cite only a few.
Of special interest is the work of CLARK and HAVILAND (CLARK, 1973b; CLARK
and HAVILAND, 1977; HAVILAND and CLARK, 1974) because they specify the role
of old and new information in the comprehension process. Comprehension has been
described by these authors in terms of the given-new contract between speaker
and listener. According to this contract the speaker expresses as given information that information which he thinks the listener already knows and as
new information that information which he thinks the listener does not yet
know. There is a variety of syntactic ways for doing so. The comprehension

process, then, is a process in which the listener identifies given and new information as such, searches memory to find an antecedent that matches the given information, and integrates the new information with that antecedent. In these studies the given information for one sentence is given in a preceding sentence.

For a recent and detailed overview on sentence perception and sentence understanding, see LEVELT (in press).

1.4 Methodology of the Present Research

Comprehension and inferential processes are investigated in the present study from an information processing point of view. The aim of this approach is to characterize the temporal organization of the processes. The methodology of the approach consists in manipulating the material that has to be processed in the task and in measuring the reaction time (RT), i.e., the time between the moment the information is presented and the moment the answer required by the task is given. By relating the RTs to the manipulations of the material, one infers to the organization of the mental processes in the tasks. This approach has been used by DONDERS (1868) and worked out by STERNBERG (1969) as the additive factor method.

The appropriate analysis of the data in this kind of research question is the analysis of variance. There are, however, some methodological problems inherent in the use of the anlaysis of variance in RT experiments. Because of the distribution of RTs and of missing data, the analyses of variance have been performed on medians of RTs for items that are considered as replications of each other. The models described in the present study are additive models based on means of medians. When generalization beyond the language sample is required, the statistic $min \ F'$ (CLARK, 1973c) is computed. Not only the values of $min \ F'$ are reported in such cases but also the values of F_1. The reason is that $min \ F'$, just as well as F', is a conservative test in particular cases (FORSTER and DICKINSON, 1976). Moreover, the procedure to treat language material as a random factor is not above dispute (WIKE and CHURCH, 1976; CLARK et al., 1976). The interpretation of the results, however, is based on the results of $min \ F'$. With respect to the assumptions concerning the variance-covariance matrices, it should be noted that all the results reported in the present study remain significant under the Geisser-Greenhouse procedure (WINER, 1971, p. 523 ff.). Further details on the statistical analysis of the reaction time data are described by Noordman and Noordman-Vonk in NOORDMAN-VONK (1979).

1.5 Overview of the Present Study

The present study consists of three parts. Two of the aforementioned types of comprehension will be dealt with. Comprehension in the first part of this study deals with the integration of verbal information in sentences with verbal information in other sentences. The emphasis in the second part is on the comprehension of verbal information with respect to knowledge of the world. The third part also deals with the comprehension of sentences with respect to knowledge of the world. The notion of given information will be extended in this part so as to include pragmatic factors such as certain presuppositions and expectations. This information will be called background information as opposed to foreground information which is explicitly communicated in the sentence.

The three parts can also be distinghuised with respect to the verbal information that has to be processed. The first part deals with the processing of comparative sentences, the second part with the interpretation and processing of conditional sentences, and the third part with inferences of kinship terms. Each part begins with a brief summary.

Part I Processing Comparative Relations

The aim of Part I is to give a detailed description of a reasoning process. More specifically, the following questions are studied: How does coded information change over time and how does the change influence the reasoning process? To what extent is the reasoning process different for information of different degrees of complexity? To what extent is the reasoning process determined by the goal that has to be attained? Are reasoning processes with verbal problems similar to reasoning processes with pictorial problems?

The material used in these experiments consists of three-term series problems, both in verbal form (*John is smaller than Pete, Bill is bigger than Pete, who is smallest?*) and in pictorial form. The standard paradigm is to vary the delay between the presentation of the two propositions and the question. A process model has been developed for the task with no such interval; predictions have been made for the tasks with a varying time interval.

The verbal information tends to be coded in unmarked form. This coding is not established immediately but gradually, depending on the complexity of the information and on the length of the time interval. Pictorial information is coded in a different form than verbal information, but the procedures of combining the information in solving the pictorial problems are very similar to those in solving the verbal problems.

Chapter 2   Empirical Questions

A characteristic of reasoning processes is that pieces of information are
combined with each other in order to achieve a goal, e.g., to draw a conclusion, to solve a problem, to make a judgment. Incoming information has to be
stored for a certain length of time, since pieces of incoming information
have to be integrated with each other as well as with previously acquired
knowledge. All this information together then is used in attaining the goal.
The processing of the information and the solving of the problem go hand in
hand, i.e., the way the information is stored has consequences for the use
of the information in solving the problem.

The general purpose of the present study is to give a desription of a
reasoning process so characterized. More specifically the following four
problems are discussed:

1) How is information coded and how does the stored information change
    over time?
2) How is the process of combining the information to be characterized,
    and to what extent does this process differ for information of differ-
    ent degrees of complexity?
3) To what extent is the reasoning process determined by the goal that has
    to be attained?
4) Are reasoning processes with verbal problems similar to reasoning pro-
    cesses with pictorial problems?

These questions deserve some further amplification.

1) *Coding of the information.* From studies on memory for sentences there
is substantial evidence that the more fully the information is processed,
the less syntactic and the more semantic or eventually conceptual the code
of the information will be. The syntactic properties of the surface structure of a sentence are retained only for a short time after the presentation
of the sentence, just long enough to analyze the meaning of the sentence
(SACHS, 1967). After a certain interval only the meaning of the sentence is

retained; sentence memory is seen as a storage of rather abstract semantic information. Many authors have studied the format of this information. Much of the work of CLARK (1974) is aimed at characterizing the underlying semantic information that is stored. FLORES d'ARCAIS (1974a) argues that a case grammar offers a good characterization of the material given in recall. He suggests that the cases are close to fundamental relations expressed in sentences. A similar point is made by RUMELHART et al. (1972), NORMAN and RUMELHART (1975), and by KINTSCH (1974). Other authors have produced evidence for the position that the coded information is an abstract base of knowledge that is not completely specified by the linguistic input (BRANSFORD et al., 1972; FRANKS and BRANSFORD, 1972; JOHNSON-LAIRD, 1974b; JOHNSON-LAIRD and STEVENSON, 1970). For an overview of research on memory for sentences see also FILLENBAUM (1973) and JOHNSON-LAIRD (1974a). All the evidence points to the conclusion that the longer the time to process a sentence, the deeper the information is processed and the more conceptual the stored information will be.

The same position is held by CRAIK and LOCKHART (1972). They propose a framework for memory research different from the models that distinguish different memory stores: sensory store, short-term store, and long-term store. They propose instead a concept of memory in which the level of processing of the information is a central notion. Information is analyzed in a series of processing stages that differ in depth. The characteristics of the memory trace depend on the level of processing the information. Greater depth is defined as a greater degree of semantic or cognitive analysis. Because man is mainly concerned with meaning, it is useful to store information in this semantic or cognitive form.

If the depth of processing of the information determines the reasoning process, factors that influence the depth of processing will have an effect on the characteristics of the reasoning process as well. One such factor is the time available to store and transform the information. Another factor is the complexity of the information. Both factors are expected to have a comparable effect on the reasoning process, more specifically on the coding of the information. The less time available or the more complex the information, the less likely it is that the information will be coded in the ultimate semantic or conceptual form. One also may expect that the amount of time available will influence the effect of the complexity. This leads to the second question in this study: In what way does the complexity of the information determine the reasoning process?

10

2) *Complexity of the information.* This question will be treated especially with respect to syntactic complexity: the same information will be presented in syntactic formats that differ in complexity. One can argue that the more complex the information, the more time is needed to code the information in a semantic or conceptual way. Consequently, the more complex the information, the more important the syntactic variables will be in characterizing the reasoning process. The difference due to syntactic complexity will disappear when there is enough time to fully process the information.

There is, however, another aspect. The complexity of the information can be an important factor in selecting a certain strategy. The more complex the information, the more likely a strategy is selected that reduces the cognitive strain. In one of their studies on concept attainment, BRUNER et al. (1956) distinguished a focussing strategy from a scanning strategy. Focussing is described as a process in which the first positive instance is used by the subject as a focus. Instances are selected that differ from the focus in only one attribute, in order to test whether that attribute is crucial or not. In a scanning strategy, on the other hand, instances are selected in order to test a hypothesis on the concept. As much information as possible about the instances is remembered, in order to use that information when testing a new hypothesis in case the present hypothesis has to be rejected. The scanning strategy imposes a higher degree of strain on memory and in- ference capacities than the focussing strategy. An experiment of BRUNER et al. was performed under two conditions. In the first condition the in- stances that could be selected were put in front of the subject. In the second condition the stimulus cards were removed. In the second condition the task is more complex than in the first condition; it imposes more strain on the problem solver. When subjects used the focussing strategy, performance in the two conditions was about the same. However, when using the scanning strategy, performance in the second condition was much poorer than in the first one. Thus, when the cognitive demands of a task are heavy, a strategy which puts less strain on memory is relatively more advantageous than a strategy that requires much memory activity.

Similarly, NEWELL, SIMON, and GREENO (GREENO and SIMON, 1974; NEWELL and SIMON, 1972; SIMON and NEWELL, 1971) argued that one of the criteria in the selection of a search strategy is the reduction of memory load. In solving complex problems humans prefer a strategy that is in itself less efficient but requires less memory load over a more efficient but more demanding strat- egy. In the progressive deepening strategy (DE GROOT, 1965) linear searches without any branches are made from the same base position, going as deeply

as necessary to evaluate the outcome of the search. This strategy reduces
the memory load because only one position needs to be stored; this can be
done in terms of the way it differs from the base position. The search-scan
strategy, on the other hand, is in itself more efficient. The node that is
most promising is selected for continuation; a few continuations from that
node are made; new nodes are evaluated and selected for continuation. In
this strategy, however, large amounts of time are needed to store information from prior nodes in long-term memory.

3) *Goal directedness*. The third question refers to the goal that has to
be reached. Thinking is goal-oriented. The characteristics of the problem
to be solved determine the course of the reasoning process (KÜLPE, 1912).
The task leads to a schematic anticipation of the solution (SELZ, 1913) and
exerts a determining tendency (ACH, 1905) that controls the thinking process and selects appropriate operations (see also FRIJDA and ELSHOUT, 1976).
The goal-oriented characteristics of the thinking process have been extensively discussed in NEWELL and SIMON (1972). The specific question in this part
of the study is: To what extent does the goal to be reached determine what
information is analyzed and in what order? If, during the process of assim-
ilating incoming information, it is already known which goal has to be attained, it is possible to analyze the information in function of that goal.
The information may then be analyzed selectively instead of exhaustively.
This will reduce the complexity of the processing. In this way the third
question is related to the second.

4) *Verbal and pictorial information*. The fourth question in this part
deals with the problem of to what extent processing verbal information is
similar to processing pictorial information. Incoming information generally
has the format of verbal messages or visual displays. Many authors have
studied the relationship between these different kinds of incoming information (BOWER, 1972; CLARK et al., 1973; MOYER, 1973; PAIVIO, 1971; SEYMOUR,
1973, 1974a, 1974b). In this framework, two specific topics will be discussed.
The first refers to the way in which verbal and pictorial information is
coded in memory. Some authors (PAIVIO, 1971, 1974) claim that it depends on
the task as to whether the information is coded in a verbal or in an imaginal
way. According to other authors (HUTTENLOCHER and HIGGINS, 1971, 1972;
SEYMOUR, 1973) the information is best characterized by imagery factors.
Finally, some authors (CLARK and CHASE, 1972; ANDERSON and BOWER, 1973;
PYLYSHYN, 1973) claim that verbal information as well as pictorial information is transformed into underlying elementary semantic propositions.
BENJAFIELD and DOAN (1971) argue that there is a common representation modus

for visual and verbal information. The second topic refers to the characteristics of the combinatorial processes in the processing of verbal and pictorial information. The question is to what extent these combinatorial processes are similar. These topics will give some insight into the relationship between verbal and pictorial reasoning. At the same time these questions touch upon the problem of the role of imagery in reasoning. That
problem has been discussed by CLARK (1969a, 1971, 1972b, 1974), HUTTENLOCHER
and HIGGINS (1971, 1972), and SHAVER et al. (1975) concerning one particular task. It should be noted, however, that, if a similarity is found between processing verbal information and processing pictorial information,
this of course does not prove that verbal reasoning is an imagery process.
It is not the aim of this study to settle the question to what extent verbal
reasoning is an imagery process.

2.1 Theories About Three-Term Series Problems

The four questions will be studied using reasoning tasks termed linear syllogisms, or three-term series problems, such as: *John is bigger than Pete, Bill
is smaller than Pete, who is smallest?* or *Marc is not as small as Paul, Paul
is not as small as Dave, who is biggest?*. Parenthetically, the sentence
Marc is not as small as Paul is not the negation of *Marc is as small as Paul*;
the "not as" specifies a direction and means "less". In the first proposition of a three-term series problem a relationship between two terms is
specified. In the second proposition the relationship between a new term
and one of the old terms is specified. In order to answer the question, these
two relations have to be integrated. Three-term series problems with negative
sentences are called negative equatives; three-term series problems with
positive sentences are called comparatives. By varying the adjective in the
first proposition, in the second proposition, and in the question, and by
varying the order of the propositions, one obtains 16 comparative and 16
negative equative items (Table 3.1). The antonym pair that has been used was
the Dutch equivalent for *big/small*, which is an unmarked-marked adjective
pair. Unmarked and marked adjectives differ in the following respect. Unmarked adjectives can be used in a neutral sense, e.g., *how good was the
film?*, as well as in a contrastive sense, e.g., *the film was good*; marked
adjectives can only be used in a contrastive sense, e.g., *the film was
bad*. For more details, see Chap. 12.
    A great deal of research has been conducted on the comprehension of com-
parative constructions (CARPENTER, 1974; CLARK, 1970a; CLARK and CARD, 1969;

FLORES d'ARCAIS, 1966, 1970, 1974b) and on three-term series problems
(CLARK, 1969a, 1969b, 1971, 1972b; DE SOTO et al., 1965; HUNTER, 1957;
HUTTENLOCHER and HIGGINS, 1971, 1972; JONES, 1970; POTTS and SCHOLZ, 1975;
QUINTON and FELLOWS, 1975; SHAVER et al., 1975). A brief summary of the main
principles proposed by these authors to account for the reasoning process
will be given here. For a more detailed overview of the theories and for a
discussion of the controversy between these theories, the reader is referred
to JOHNSON-LAIRD (1972).

The linguistic theory of CLARK specifies three principles that govern the
reasoning process. According to one principle - the primacy of functional
relations - a comparative sentence such as *John is better than Bill* is coded
as (John is good +) (Bill is good). The information of the two underlying
subject-predicate relationships is more readily available than the information of the comparative itself. According to the principle of lexical
marking, unmarked adjectives such as *good* and *long* are psychologically less
complex than marked adjectives such as *bad* and *short*. The principle of
congruence states that a problem is easier when the underlying representation
of the question is the same as the underlying representation of the information asked for than when they are different. Thus, for the item *John is
better than Bill*, the question *who is best?* is easier than the question
who is worst? For the item *John is better than Pete, Bill is worse than
Pete* both questions are easier than for the item *Pete is better than Bill,
Pete is worse than John*. The first item is called a congruent item. The
answer to the question *who is best?* is coded in terms of the adjective of
the question: *better*; similarly, the answer to the question *who is worst?*
is coded in terms of the adjective of the question: *worse*. This is not the
case for the second item, which is, therefore, called an incongruent item.
Finally for some items CLARK postulates an additional principle: the compressing strategy. This strategy deals with the integration of the two propositions. The proposition *John is better than Bill* is compressed into
(John is good +). If this proposition is followed by *Marc is better than
John*, it is easier to construct the three-term series than if the second
proposition is *Bill is better than Steve*, because in the first case the information retained from the first proposition can serve as point of reference for the second proposition.

These principles specify the way in which the information is coded as
well as some consequences for the retrieval of the information. CLARK, however, does not give a detailed description of the reasoning process as such.

An earlier theory which leads to different predictions was proposed by
HUNTER (1957). The propositions are transformed in such a way that the result
is either *John is better than Pete, Pete is better than Bill* or *Bill is worse
than Pete, Pete is worse than John*. There are two operations that are used
to obtain this result: converting the order of the terms in a proposition
and reordering the propositions. The need to apply these operations determines the relative difficulty of the problems.

Other authors emphasize the importance of imagery and spatial ordering in
solving three-term series problems. According to the spatial paralogic theory of DE SOTO et al. (1965), the subject constructs a visual image of the
three-term series. This construction is easier when it is built from the top
down than when it is built working up from the bottom. Thus *A is bigger than
B, B is bigger than C* is easier than *C is worse than B, B is worse than A*
(by convention, A denotes the biggest person and C the smallest person). A
second principle states that the information in a proposition will be easier
to represent in the visual image when its first term is an "end-anchor"
(i.e., A or C) than when it is the middle term (B): the image is easier to
construct from the extremes inward than from the middle outward.

HUTTENLOCHER (1968) proposes an alternative explanation of the end-anchoring effect. According to HUTTENLOCHER, a subject will arrange the three-term
series into a mental array similar to the way in which he arranges physical
objects. Thus, when the subject has to place a movable object, i.e., an object he has in his hand, with respect to a fixed object, i.e., an object put
in front of him, the task is easier when the movable object is described as
the first term, the grammatical subject, of the comparative sentence than
when it is described as the second term of the comparative sentence. The
parallel of these overt arrangement tasks with the covert processes in solving three-term series problems is that the new term in the second proposition is treated as a movable object. HUTTENLOCHER states that if the new
term is the first term in the second proposition, the problem is easier than
when the new term is the second term in the second proposition.

In concluding, the theories about reasoning with three-term series problems may be distinguished on the basis of what they claim with respect to
the coding of the information. The linguistic theory claims that the information is coded in a propositional format. The imagery theory postulates that
the information is coded in the form of mental images. Some other studies
relate to the image theory in the sense that they focussed on the representation of the scale underlying linear ordering (GRIGGS and SHEA, 1977;
POLICH and POTTS, 1977; POTTS, 1972, 1974; TRABASSO and RILEY, 1975). In many

of these studies, four or more term series have been used and inferences
from the underlying representation have been studied.

2.2 Some Empirical Evidence

JONES (1970) has tested the spatial paralogic theory of DE SOTO et al. against
the linguistic theory of CLARK. The predictions of the spatial paralogic theory were based on the results of an independent experiment in which subjects
made spatial assignments to the terms in comparative and negative equative
sentences. The linguistic theory gave a better prediction of the relative
difficulty of the items than the spatial paralogic theory.

The merits of the imagery theory of HUTTENLOCHER and of the linguistic theory of CLARK have been extensively discussed (CLARK, 1969a, 1971, 1972a, 1972b,
HUTTENLOCHER and HIGGINS, 1971, 1972). Although the two theories differ sub-
stantially in their description of the reasoning processes, they make the
same predictions of the relative difficulty of the items, as long as one assumes that a negative sentence such as *John isn't as good as Pete* is transformed into *Pete is better than John*. This reconciliation has also been discussed
by JOHNSON-LAIRD (1972). The stumbling block for the image theory was in fact
the observation that a negative equative item is easier when the new term is
not the first term but the second term in the second proposition. This result,
however, does not invalidate the image theory; much to the contrary, it is in
complete agreement with that theory if the previously described transformation takes place. The theory of HUTTENLOCHER admits this transformation, although the authors claim that it is not a universal principle in the processing of negative equatives (HUTTENLOCHER and HIGGINS, 1971, p.495; 1972,
p.421). This transformation is also in agreement with the theory of CLARK.
He implicitly postulates the occurrence of this transformation in reasoning
processes (not however in the task termed "pure placement task" to be discussed later in which an object has to be placed). The proposition *John isn't
as bad as Pete* is coded as (John is bad) (Pete is bad +); the sentence *Pete
is worse than John* is coded in exactly the same underlying base strings.

As far as the predictions of the image theory are concerned, but not its
"major strength" as HUTTENLOCHER and HIGGINS claim (1971, p.498), this theory could just as well be called a "presuppositional" theory. According to
the image theory, an item such as *John is worse than Pete, Bill is better
than Pete* should be easier than an item such as *Pete is worse than John,
Pete is better than Bill*: when the new term in the second proposition (Bill)
is subject, the task is easier than when the new term is not subject. The ex-

planation was derived from tasks in which three objects had to be arranged physically: the same mental operations are assumed to be involved. The same prediction can be made, however, on the basis of the surface structure of the sentences. The second proposition of the second item given above specifies the relative goodness of Pete with respect to the goodness of Bill. According to that proposition the goodness of Bill is the point of reference and is presupposed to be known, otherwise the sentence would be odd. However, Bill is the unknown term, whereas Pete is already known from the first proposition. Pete is the actual reference point in the comparison. So, there is an incongruence between what is actually old and new information with what is according to the structure of the sentence old and new information. So the sentence *Pete is better than Bill* has to be elaborated upon in order to find out the relative goodness of Bill with respect to Pete. The incongruence between what information is actually old and new and what information is old and new according to the sentence structure is not present in the first of the items just mentioned. In this way, the predictions of the image theory are a variant of the given-new strategy proposed by CLARK (1973b; CLARK and HAVILAND, 1977).

Evidence from pure placement tasks: challenging the image theory? The discussion between CLARK and HUTTENLOCHER concerns not so much the differential predictions of the processes in deductive reasoning as the parallel between reasoning processes and placement tasks. CLARK presents one kind of experiments, the pure placement tasks, in which the results differ from those of the reasoning experiments (CLARK, 1970a, 1971, 1972a, 1972b). In these pure placement tasks, a subject read a sentence like *A is not as low as B*. He then saw an array containing the objects B and C. He had to determine which term of the sentence was the new term and then to place the new term into the array. Not only the comparative items but also the negative equative items were easier when the new term was the subject of the sentence than when the new term functioned as the reference point in that sentence. This result was also found with children (VAN DEN BOS, 1974). Thus, in these tasks subjects do not reorganize a sentence *A is not as low as B* into *B is lower than A*. This discrepancy between pure placement tasks and reasoning tasks led CLARK to reject the image theory which postulates a parallel between the two tasks. However, one may ask whether the difference between the results in the two tasks should be attributed to the nature of the tasks - placement vs reasoning tasks - or perhaps to the nature of the questions to be answered. On closer inspection, the tasks are not quite comparable as far as the instructions and the questions are concerned. This difference may be responsible for a difference in strategy between the two tasks. In the placement task one has to decide which object is new and to place the new object with respect to the old ones. In the reasoning tasks one has to construct the three-term series and to decide which term is highest or lowest. Suppose that in a placement task a red, a green, and a blue object have to be located with respect to each other in this way:

Red

Green

Blue

Assume that on a given trial the green object is presented above the blue object and that the sentence is *red is not as low as green*. Then, it is very unlikely that this sentence will be transformed into the sentence *green is lower than red*. The reason is that in *red is not as low as green* there is a congruence between what is old information according to the structure of the sentence and what is actually old information. It is unlikely that this congruent sentence is transformed into the incongruent sentence *green is lower than red*. For the same reason one has to assume that the incongruent sentence *green is not as high as red* is transformed into the congruent sentence *red is higher than green*.

Now two questions have to be answered. First, one has to explain the results of the placement task: sentences in which the new term is subject are easier than sentences in which the new term is not subject. Assuming that the above specified transformations are made, one has to explain that the transformation of the incongruent sentence *green is not as high as red* into the congruent sentence *red is higher than green* takes more time than the transformation of the congruent sentence *red is not as low as green* into the congruent sentence *red is higher than green*. This difference can be accounted for by postulating that the first step in the transformation is the search for the new term and that, if the new term is the first term of the sentence, it is available more quickly than if the new term is the second term in the sentence. It should be noted that the two transformations also differ in another respect. The first transformation changes the order of the terms; the adjective remains the same. The second transformation is a change of the adjective and not of the order of the terms. The observation that the order is harder to change than the adjective might be explained in the way just described.

The second question concerns the difference between the reasoning tasks and the placement tasks. Is this difference due to the nature of the tasks - implicit vs explicit placement processes - or to different strategies induced

by the instruction as suggested above? The question, therefore, is whether
the results of the placement tasks can be found in a reasoning task with a
modification of the instruction. The following experiment should be done.
Present the first proposition and then the second proposition with the instruction that the subject has to decide which term is the new term and to
locate this term with respect to the old terms.

The aim of these remarks is not to decide in favor of either the imagery
theory or the linguistic theory. Review of more evidence would be necessary,
e.g., from a more detailed study of the combinatorial processes and from the
results on indeterminate cases. The point, however, is to demonstrate that
it is quite plausible that sentences like *A is not as big as B* are transformed into *B is bigger than A*. More generally, it is suggested that the way
a negative sentence is transformed depends possibly more on the requirements
of the task than on the fact as to whether the task is a reasoning task or a
placement task. It is suggested that the aforementioned negative transformation occurs in certain reasoning taks as well as in certain placement tasks.

Evidence on the unified representation: challenging the linguistic theory?
The discussion between CLARK and HUTTENLOCHER actually referred largely to
the question whether or not verbal reasoning has the same characteristics as
placement tasks. However, even a discrepancy between the two tasks does not
necessarily invalidate the image theory of reasoning. The discrepancy can be
accounted for by factors other than the difference between imagery and verbal
factors, as has been argued above. However, it is possible to contrast both
theories; there are in fact differences between the two. The theories differ
in what they specify about the storage and the integration of the information.
The critical difference between the two theories is, according to JOHNSON-LAIRD
(1972), whether subjects make a unified representation of the information in
the propositions. Moreover, he suggests that subjects, in solving the first
few items, make such a representation, but that they very soon, after perhaps
only two or three items, shift to a more linguistic strategy. However, the
construction of a unified representation is a critical difference only in
that CLARK (1969a) does not specify how the integration of the information
is made. This is in fact a gap in this theory. But this does not mean that
CLARK claims that an integration is not made. One can hardly conceive of a
solution in which that representation has not been made in one form or another. In other studies CLARK argues that sentences and pictures are coded in
a similar underlying system of semantic elements. In that perspective one can
hardly maintain that CLARK denies that a unified representation is made in
three-term series problem solving. In fact, the critical question is not

whether a unified representation of the information is made or not, but whether that representation can best be described by imagery or by linguistic factors. The research of linear orderings, referred to earlier, is relevant in this respect.

A study of POTTS and SCHOLZ (1975) is concerned with the internal representation of three-term series problems. Also according to these authors, the basis of the controversy between HUTTENLOCHER and CLARK is the question of whether a unified representation is made and what the characteristics of that representation are. The results of that study will not be discussed now, only the interpretation of the results as far as the linguistic theory is concerned. The main conclusions of that paper are that there is a kind of integration of the information in the propositions and that the information is stored in unmarked form. The suty of POTTS and SCHOLZ and some of the experiment to be reported in the present study used, independently from each other, the same paradigm.For problems in which the two propositions used the same adjective, there is no interaction between the adjective of the question and the adjective of the propositions when the question is presented after the propositions. It is not found that the RT is shorter when the adjectives of the question and of the propositions are the same than when they are different. Instead, there was a main effect of the adjective of the question: the RT for the question *who is best?* was shorter than for the question *who is worst?*. This can be considered as evidence that the information is coded in unmarked form. The linguistic theory claims, according to POTTS and SCHOLZ, that the marked and unmarked adjectives are coded as such and that consequently there had to be an interaction between the adjective of the propositions and the adjective of the question. Another result was that the time to process the incongruent propositions such as *B is better than C, B is worse than A* was longer than the time to process the congruent propositions such as *A is better than B, C is worse than B*. This led POTTS and SCHOLZ to the conclusion that there is a kind of integration of the information as HUTTENLOCHER claims. The linguistic theory, according to POTTS and SCHOLZ, only postulates that marked adjectives are harder to process than unmarked adjectives. So the prediction from that theory would be that the RTs for the congruent and incongruent items do not differ because in both cases there is one marked adjective involved. This refutation of the linguistic theory seems questionable, however. In general one can conclude that the results obtained from Potts and Scholz's study against the linguistic theory of CLARK are indeed not predicted by his theory. These results, however, are not in conflict with the linguistic theory and might even perfectly fit into an extended version of a linguistic theory. First, that the information is coded in unmarked form does in no way conflict with Clark's theory. Contrarily, in a memory experiment (CLARK and CARD, 1969) it was found that the adjective *bad* is reproduced as *good* more often than *good* is reproduced as *bad*. Thus, *good* seems to be a more basic notion than *bad* (CLARK, 1974). This supports the idea that there is a tendency to code the information in unmarked form. So one can argue that the information is coded initially in the adjective of the propositions and finally in unmarked form. Therefore, the difference between the results of the POTTS and SCHOLZ experiments where the question is presented after the propositions and where the question is presented simultaneously with the propositions does not necessarily exclude the possibility, as POTTS and SCHOLZ claim, that in the latter case the propositions are analyzed before the question. Secondly, CLARK does not specify any prediction with respect to the time needed to understand the congruent and the incongruent propositions. This does not mean, however, that he predicts that there is no difference: on the contrary, the fact that the time to understand the congruent propositions is shorter than the time to understand the incongruent propositions does not conflict with Clark's theory. In fact, one might argue that the congruent items are congruent with the actual placements of the terms, as POTTS and SCHOLZ admit. It is possible that in understanding the propositions, one anticipates the question *who is best?* and *who is worst?*. Consequently, the RT for the congruent items is shorter than for the incongruent items, because in the former case the information stored and the information asked for are coded in the same way. For example, in the item *A is better than B, C is worse than B* A is coded as good + and C as bad +. In the item *B is worse than A, B is better than C* however, B is coded good + as well as bad +. It is only indirectly that one will detect A and C as the extremes. This explanation fits with Clark's principle of congruence. Another reason why, according to an extended linguistic theory, the time to understand the congruent propositions is shorter than the time to understand the incongruent propositions has been given earlier: in the incongruent propositions there is an incongruence between what is old and new information according to the structure of the sentence and what is actually old and new information. Summarizing, the results of the study of POTTS and SCHOLZ are that a unified representation is made of the propositions, and that the information is finally coded in unmarked form. These results do not conflict with an extended linguistic theory of reasoning. But as stated above, the study of POTTS and SCHOLZ did not focus primarily on the distinction between imagery and linguistic processes in reasoning, but more on the role of the unified representation of the information.

Evidence on imagery: challenging the linguistic theory? A study which is centrally concerned with the role of imagery in three-term series problems has been carried out by SHAVER et al. (1975). They presented the following evidence for the use of imagery in problem solving. Problems with spatial relations (e.g., *above, below*) were easier to solve than problems with nonspatial relations (e.g., *lighter, darker*). When the problems were presented in a reading condition which is assumed to interfere with imagery, they were more difficult to solve than when presented in a listening condition. This difference was greater for the problems with spatial relations than for the problems with nonspatial relations. The correlation between scores on a test of spatial reasoning and errors on problem solving was highest (with negative sign) for the most difficult problems, the nonspatial problems. Finally, when instructed to use an image strategy, subjects made less errors than control subjects. The authors conclude that imagery plays a functional role in the solution of three-term series problems. Contrary to JOHNSON-LAIRD, SHAVER et al. conclude that subjects might abandon the linguistic strategy in favor of an image strategy.

However, a number of critical remarks can be made with respect to the results. First, the assumption that reading interferes with imagery is questionable (ANDERSON and BOWER, 1973, p.459; PYLYSHYN, 1973). Consequently, it is questionable whether the poorer performance in the reading condition than in the listening condition is due to the interference with imagery. The peculiarities of the mode of presentation in the reading condition might be an alternative explanation, as SHAVER et al. indicate. Secondly, the interpretation of the interaction between reading vs listening condition and relation type is questionable for the same reason as just stated. Moreover, that interaction is only marginally significant by conventional standards ($p < 0.10$). Thirdly, the interpretation of the correlations between spatial reasoning scores and errors in problem solving is problematic. If spatial reasoning ability differentiates best between subjects' problem solving performance in the difficult conditions, then the correlation between spatial reasoning and errors should be higher (with negative sign), the more difficult the condition. This is not found. The Spearman relationship between these correlations and the difficulty, reconstructed from the data given, is only -0.37.

It is argued that the correlation between errors and spatial reasoning scores must be higher in the easier listening condition, which leads to the use of imagery, than in the reading condition. But if this is correct one should expect that the correlations are also high in other situations that favor the use of imagery, e.g., when solving spatial problems. This is not the case. For example, the correlation for spatial problems in the reading condition is lower than for the nonspatial problems in the reading condition. So one has to explain why one factor that enhances the use of imagery, namely the listening condition, raises the correlation between spatial reasoning and errors, while another factor that enhances the use of imagery, namely problems with spatial relations, does not raise the correlation. The predictions with respect to the correlations between errors and spatial reasoning seem to lack a coherent theoretical basis.

2.3 Concluding Remarks

Some theories about reasoning with three-term series problems have been discussed, emphasizing the linguistic theory and the imagery theory. No decision with respect to the correctness of these theories was made. Much of the alleged evidence favoring the one or the other theory did not seem to be conclusive. As far as the empirical predictions of the theories are concerned, it was argued that the theories can easily be reconciled with each other.

The aim of the present study is not to test empirically the linguistic theory and the imagery theory, but to give a detailed description of a reasoning process focussing on the general problems discussed in the beginning of this chapter. This objective has determined the selection of the experimental material and paradigms: three-term series problems seemed appropriate for the study of these questions. The theories that have been discussed serve as a starting point for the present research; the effects that are postulated by these theories constitute hypotheses about the reasoning process in the present study.

In this part six experiments will be discussed. The first four deal with verbal three-term series problems, the other two with pictorial three-term series problems.[1]

---

[1] Some of the experiments and the model to be discussed were presented at the International Meeting of the Experimental Psychology Society and the Netherlands Psychonomics Foundation, Cambridge, July 1975.

Chapter 3 A Model for Solving Verbal Problems

In the first experiment the question is presented together with the propositions. The time necessary to produce the answer is measured. In Experiment II the item is divided into two parts. First, the two propositions are presented. The time necessary to understand the propositions is measured; this time will be referred to as the inspection time (RTi). Then the question is presented and the time necessary to answer the question is measured; this time will be called the answering time (RTa). Experiments III and IV are similar to the previous one: both inspection time and answering time are measured. The difference is that there is a blank interval of 4 and 8 s, respectively, after the inspection time before the question is presented.

The experimental paradigms are related to the questions to be studied in the following way. The first problem to be discussed in this part is how information is coded and stored over a certain time period. In the present experiments the time period over which the information of the propositions has to be retained increases from Experiment I to Experiments II, III, IV. The second problem is how the complexity of the information affects the reasoning process and whether differences due to complexity of the material decrease when the information has to be stored over time. The material in the present experiments consists of comparative items and negative equative items, the latter being more complex than the former. The third problem concerns the relation between the question and the propositions. Only in Experiment I is the question presented simultaneously with the propositions. If the question influences the reasoning process, the results in Experiment I should differ from those in Experiments II, III, and IV.

3.1 Experiment I

3.1.1 Method

Material. The 32 item types used in the experiments are presented in Table 3.1. The letters stand for boys' names. Three items have been constructed for each type, yielding a total of 96 experimental items. An item consisted

Table 3.1. Mean latencies [ms] for the three-term series problems in Experiment I

		Form of propositions	Form of question	
			biggest?	smallest?
I	a	A bigger than B; B bigger than C	6518	6719
	b	B bigger than C; A bigger than B	6239	6800
II	a	C smaller than B; B smaller than A	7309	7544
	b	B smaller than A; C smaller than B	7763	7385
III	a	A bigger than B; C smaller than B	7167	6655
	b	C smaller than B; A bigger than B	6946	7191
IV	a	B smaller than A; B bigger than C	6875	7014
	b	B bigger than C; B smaller than A	6393	7934
I'	a	A not as small as B; B not as small as C	7995	7339
	b	B not as small as C; A not as small as B	9115	8808
II'	a	C not as big as B; B not as big as A	6513	8118
	b	B not as big as A; C not as big as B	8783	9175
III'	a	A not as small as B; C not as big as B	9297	7971
	b	C not as big as B; A not as small as B	8125	9346
IV'	a	B not as big as A; B not as small as C	8049	7920
	b	B not as small as C; B not as big as A	7872	8142

of the two propositions, the question, and the three names as answer alternatives ordered in a row. The items have been constructed by first selecting a large number (26) of common boys' names of three letters each. Three names occurred in only one item together; a pair of names occurred in at most two items together. No names which can easily be confused with each other, i.e., names with two consecutive identical letters or with the same first letter, occurred in an item. The correct answer was an equal number of times the left middle, and right boy's name in the row of the answer alternatives. Moreover, special attention was given to the distribution of the names in the item. The names were equated as much as possible with respect to a number of characteristics of occurrence: each name was an equal number of times the B-term, i.e., the term that is mentioned twice in an item; each name was approximatel the same number of times the answer to the question *who is biggest?* and also to the question *who is smallest?*; the frequency of occurrence as first, second, and third name in an item was approximately equal for each name; the name that is the correct answer occurred an approximately equal number of times as first, second, and third term in the item.

The experimental items have been divided into 6 blocks of 16 items each, in such a way that two blocks together contained the set of 32 items of Table 3.1. Each block contained 8 positive (comparative) and 8 negative (negative equative) items; 8 items with the question *who is biggest?* and 8 with the question *who is smallest?*; 8 items with the same adjective in the two propositions (homogeneous items) and 8 items with different adjectives in the two propositions (heterogeneous items); the blocks were balanced also with respect to the interaction of these three factors. The first, second, and third name in the item was the answer for an approximately equal number of items in each block. A name occurred approximately an equal number of times in each block. A particular name did not occur more than once in three consecutive items. Apart from the experimental blocks there was one practice block that was in all respects similar to the experimental blocks. One practice item was added to each block as the first item of the block, so that there were in total 7 blocks of 17 items each.

Subjects. The subjects were 22 students of different disciplines. The age of the students was on the average 23 years, varying from 20 to 26 years. The subjects volunteered in the experiment; they were paid for their participation.

Procedure. The items were presented by means of two Leitz Pradovit projectors, equipped with electronic Furth shutters, adapted for this kind of experiment. The two propositions, the question and the answer alternatives were presented by means of one projector; the other projector projected a blank field during the time interval between the items. The subject was sitting in a soundproof room at a distance of 2.15 m from the screen. The sentences were clearly visible as black letters on a white field. The positive propositions subtended a visual angle of approximately 11 deg; the negative propositions subtended a visual angle of approximately 14 deg. All the equipment was in a room next to the subject's room; the items were projected through a plan-parallel coated glass window in the wall. The shutters and the projectors were controlled by two control units especially devised for this equipment. The time was measured by a Hewlett-Packard time-counter (HP 5300/5304A).

The subject was instructed to answer the question as quickly as possible without making errors. The answer was given by pressing a button to be selected from a row of three buttons; there was a 5 cm distance between two buttons. The subject was told that the position of the buttons in the row corresponded to the position of the answer alternatives on the slide. The buttons had to be pressed with the index finger of the dominant hand; this finger remained on a fixed central location during the experiment except when the answer had to be executed. The time was measured from the onset of the presentation until the subject pressed the button. There was a 4 s interval between two items. Between two blocks of items there was an interval of approximately 1 min. At the beginning and the end of each block the subject was given an auditory warning signal. The experiment lasted about 40 min.

After the experiment the subject was asked some questions about the way he had solved the problems. In collecting these introspective data the subject was presented with some problems, each being typed on a separate card. The subject was asked to specify as precisely as possible how he had solved the problems.

3.1.2 Results

As a rule, subjects with a large number of errors relative to the distribution of errors are not included in the analysis. In the present experiment four subjects made more than 9% of errors; they were eliminated from the analysis. The percentage of errors for the 22 remaining subjects was on the average 3%.

For each of these subjects 32 medians for the correct answers have been computed, one median for each item type. A one-way analysis of variance with repeated measures has been performed on these medians. The means of these medians are presented in Table 3.1. Based on the theories of CLARK, HUTTENLOCHER and DE SOTO, discussed in Chap. 2, and on some previous pilot studies, a great number of possibly important factors had been specified. These factors define contrasts between mean RTs of groups of items. The main contrasts that have been computed are presented in Table 3.2. These contrasts have been computed for comparative items and for negative equative items separately. Many contrasts have been computed separately for homogeneous and heterogeneous items and for items with a marked and with an unmarked adjective in the first or second proposition or in the question.

Table 3.2. Main contrasts between items computed in the present experiments

negative equatives	-comparatives
heterogeneous	-homogeneous
marked	-unmarked adjective first proposition
marked	-unmarked adjective second proposition
new term is point of reference-subject in second propostion	
question incongruent	-congruent with coded information[a]
disfavored	-favored by compressing strategy
nonlinear	-linear[b]
adjective question different	-same as adjective first proposition
adjective question different	-same as adjective second proposition
answer in first	-in second proposition
question *smallest?*	*-biggest?*

[a] According to the linguistic theory.

[b] Linear items are items in which the order of the terms is A, B, C or C, B, A.

These contrasts are of course not all mutually independent. The following effects that are defined by mutually independent comparisons account for all the observed differences. The RT for negative equative items is 1257 ms longer than for comparative items: $t(651) = 8.48$, $p < 0.001$. There is a marked-unmarked effect for comparative items, but not for negative equative items: the RT for items with a marked adjective is longer than for items with an unmarked adjective, this difference is 450 ms for the adjective of the first proposition: $t(651) = 2.14$, $p < 0.05$ and 481 ms for the adjective of the second proposition: $t(651) = 2.29$, $p < 0.05$. The RT is 477 ms shorter when the answer occurs in the second proposition than when it occurs in the first proposition: $t(651) = 3.22$, $p < 0.01$. Although this recency effect was 392 ms for comparative items and 563 ms for negative equative items, this effect did not interact with the variable comparatives-negative equatives: $t(651) = 0.58$, $0.50 < p < 0.60$. Two more effects have been found for the negative equative items only. When the adjective of the first proposition differs from the adjective of the question the RT is 639 ms longer than when the adjectives are the same: $t(651) = 3.04$, $p < 0.01$; no such effect is found for the second proposition. Finally the RT is 1084 ms longer when the new term A or C in the second proposition is subject than when it is the reference point: $t(651)$ = 5.16, p < 0.001. This will be called the reference point-subject effect. There were no interactions between these factors. The significant comparisons are summarized in Table 3.3. This set of orthogonal comparisons accounts for 91% of the sum of squares between the 32 items.

Table 3.3. Summary of results of Experiment I

Comparison	Difference [ms]
negative equative (NE)- comparative (Comp)	1257
marked - unmarked adjective first proposition Comp	450
marked - unmarked adjective second proposition Comp	481
answer in first proposition - in second proposition	477
adjective question different - same as adjective first proposition NE	639
new term subject - point of reference NE	1084

correlation with model r = 0.95
mean RT 7656 ms

3.1.3 Discussion

On the basis of these results a model of the reasoning process has been constructed that is presented in Fig. 3.1. In this model the operations are ordered serially. Each operation requires an increment of time. These increments are considered as additive. Observed differences in RT between items are accounted for by differentiating operations in the model. These operations are the parameters of the model.

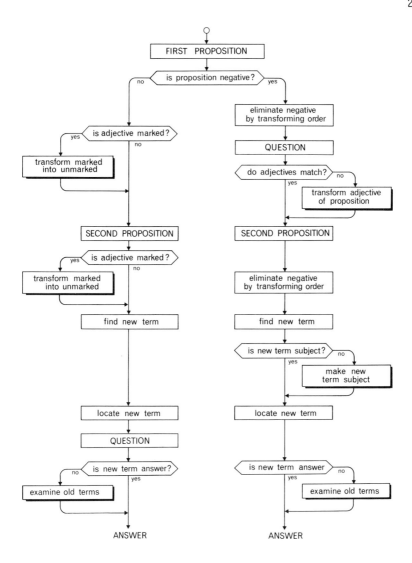

Fig. 3.1. Process model for solving three-term series problems in
Experiment I

In solving the comparatives, the relations between the two terms in the first proposition is coded in unmarked form. This requires a marked-unmarked transformation, if the adjective is marked. The same is true for the second proposition: the relation is coded in unmarked form if necessary after a marked-unmarked transformation. The extra time to solve items with two marked adjectives was indeed twice the extra time to solve items with only one marked adjective. The marked-unmarked effect for the first proposition did not interact with that of the second proposition: $t(651) = 0.06$. The new term in the second proposition is searched for, and the relation, i.e., the relative size of the new term with respect to the old ones is determined. This is indicated by "locate new term". Then the question is processed. If the answer is not the term that has just been located, one has to go back to the old terms. Apparently the new term is more available than the old terms.

The processes in the case of the negative equative items are somewhat different. After having detected the negation, the first step is to eliminate the negation by transforming the order of the terms, e.g., *Bill is not as big as Sam* becomes *Sam is bigger than Bill*. Then the question is processed and the relation between the two terms in the first proposition is specified using the adjective of the question. This requires an adjective transformation in case the adjective of the proposition is different from the adjective of the question. The negation of the second proposition is eliminated in the same way as for the first proposition. The new term is searched for and the relations, i.e., the relative size of the new term, is determined with respect to the old terms. This is indicated again by "locate new term". Suppose that at this moment the transformed second proposition is *Sam is bigger than Bill*, where Bill is the new term. According to the structure of this sentence, Bill is the reference point for Sam. However, Bill, the new term, has to be located with respect to Sam. Because of this incongruence the sentence is transformed into *Bill is smaller than Sam*. This transformation does not occur when the new term is the reference point in the original second proposition, because in eliminating the negative the new term becomes the subject. If, at this stage in the model, the answer is not the term that has just been located, one has to go back to the terms of the first proposition.

There is a clear difference between the processes with comparatives and negative equatives. The main factor in processing the comparative items is the marked-unmarked factor. It is clear that the reasoning process for the negative equatives is much more determined by the syntactic surface characteristics. By this it is not meant that the processes are characterized by the analysis of the *not as* construction; that would be trivial. The point is first, that the relations are not directly coded in the semantically simpler form of the unmarked adjective as is the case for the comparative items. Second, the information of the two propositions is combined by manipulating the grammatical role of the new term. This is not the case for the processing of the comparatives. The more laborious way of analyzing the information in the negative equatives can be attributed to the fact that the item that is projected on the screen differs from the item that is worked upon much more in case of the negative equatives than in case of the comparatives. In other words, the external memory support is less for the negative equatives than for the comparatives.

Another difference between comparatives and negative equatives concerns the role of the question in the analysis of the items. Only the negative equatives are analyzed in function of the question. The question is anticipated. If the first proposition is *John is smaller than Pete* and the question is *who is smallest?*, Pete need not be examined and remembered any more. Accordingly, analysis in function of the question reduces the amount of information to be processed. From this point of view, it makes sense that this effect is found for the more complex items, the negative equatives, and not for the comparative items. In terms of problem-solving strategies (NEWELL and SIMON, 1972) it can be concluded that the negative equatives are solved using a backward search; the comparatives are solved by a forward search, at least the data do not provide evidence for a backward search.

In the present model it is assumed that also the first proposition in the negative equative items is transformed by changing the order of the two terms: *Bill is not as big as John* is transformed into *John is bigger than Bill*. This assumption is made on two grounds. First, only one operation is necessary to account for the comprehension of the negativity in the first proposition as well as in the second proposition. Second, in that transformation, the adjective is maintained. This is required because the congruence of the adjective of the question with the adjective of the first proposition appeared to be an important factor. However, one could assume that the first proposition is transformed so that the adjective of the transformed proposition is the same as the adjective of the question. But then one has to explain why the transformation of, e.g., *John is not as small as Bill* into *Bill is smaller than John* requires less time than the transformation of *Bill is not as big as John* into *Bill is smaller than John*, when the question is *who is smallest?* and similarly why the transformation of *Bill is not as big*

as John into *John is bigger than Bill* requires less time than the transformation of *John is not as small as Bill* into *John is bigger than Bill* when
the question is *who is biggest?*. In other words, one has to explain why a
transformation of the order of the terms is easier than a transformation of
the adjective. This cannot be accounted for by the mechanism of old and new
information as has been suggested in the previous chapter for the second proposition, because at this moment in the analysis, there is not yet such an
old-new distinction.

It has been observed that the RT was shorter when the answer was mentioned
in the second proposition than when in the first proposition. This recency
effect is similar to results of Clark and Sengul, cited in CLARK (1978).
In a comprehension experiment, people were faster in understanding a target
sentence when the referent to which the target sentence referred had been
mentioned only one sentence before than when it had been mentioned two or
three sentences before. Such a recency effect might be accounted for by mechanisms of a push down stack, such as has been described in the MATCH processes of HAM (ANDERSON and BOWER, 1973).

The present model reconciles the image theory of HUTTENLOCHER with the
linguistic theory of CLARK as far as the predictions on three-term series
problems are concerned. The image theory has been refuted by CLARK because
the RT for negative equative items is shorter when the new term in the second
proposition is reference point than when the new term is subject. But if the
negation is eliminated by the transformation that changes the roles of subject and reference point, the RT is shorter when the new term is subject,
after that transformation.

However, the data support neither the image model of HUTTENLOCHER nor the
linguistic model of CLARK. With respect to the comparatives, both theories
predict, although on different grounds, that the so-called congruent items
are easier than the incongruent items. The data do not support this prediction. Moreover, there is no trace of a preference to work downwards as is
maintained in the image theory. There is also no evidence for the use of the
compressing strategy, advocated by CLARK. Furthermore, no support is found
for the theory of HUNTER stating that an item is easy if the three terms
are mentioned in an order corresponding to the continuum on which they are
compared.

How does one explain the differences between earlier and the present data?
The correlation between the data of CLARK (1969a) and the present data, although highly significant, is only 0.65. There are some differences in the
experimental procedures. CLARK presented an item typed on an IBM card; the

RT was measured from a signal given to the subject to indicate that he had
to turn the card. Each problem was solved three times by each subject. The
longest solution time of these three was discarded in the analysis. (The
means reported by CLARK were accordingly considerably shorter than the means
reported in Table 3.1.) But it is not clear at all to what extent these differences between the experiments might explain the differences in the data.
The reliability of the present data and of the model can best be evaluated
by continued experimentation. The experiments to be reported later serve as
such a reliability test.

The more general question about differences between subjects has not yet
been answered. Can the subjects be split into a number of different groups
of subjects in which a group is defined as those subjects who use one particular strategy? In that case the analysis of the means over subjects would
obscure the different strategies that were actually used. One can even think
of the possibility that each subject used a particular strategy different
from other subjects. Besides the RT data, the introspective reports can help
in identifying these strategies. For this purpose, the correlations between
subjects have been computed and the RTs have been analyzed by means of factor
analysis, treating the subjects as the variables. No evidence was obtained,
however, for the existence of different groups of subjects who used the same
strategy. Furthermore, the comparisons that have been mentioned above have
been computed for each subject separately. These results did not indicate
the existence of different groups of sujects either. The main finding with
respect to the introspective data was their uselessness. In almost all cases
the strategy a subject claimed to have used was not supported by his RT data.
For a discussion of the relative uselessness of this kind of introspective
data, one is referred to NISBETT and DECAMP WILSON (1977).

Another problem to be envisaged is whether subjects changed their strategy during the experiment. In order to get a rough indication of this possibility, the analysis described earlier was carried out on the first four
blocks of the experiment. This analysis yielded practically the same results
as discussed so far.

To what extent does the model account for the data? The times for the different operations in the model that differentiate between the items have been
estimated. The time estimate of such an operation or parameter is obtained by
computing the differences of the means of two groups of items that differ
only with respect to that parameter. These time estimates are presented in
Table 3.3, except the estimate for the processing of the negations, which
was 862 ms. It seemed adequate to consider the two marked-unmarked transfor-

mations as one parameter (466 ms). In fact, there was no difference between the marked-unmarked effect for the first proposition and the marked-unmarked effect for the second proposition: $t(651) = 0.10$, $0.90 < p < 0.95$. Similarly, the two operations "examine old terms" have been considered as the same operation, because there was no interaction between the presence/absence of this operation and the comparative/negative equative construction of the propositions, as has been stated earlier.

The Pearson correlation between the observed data and the data predicted by the model is 0.95; the correlation for the comparatives and negative equatives separately was 0.82 and 0.93, respectively.

One remark should be made with respect to the answering subroutine. The relations between the terms in the comparatives are coded in unmarked form. Accordingly, one would expect that the RT for the question *who is biggest?* is shorter than for the question *who is smallest?*, because the information asked for in the question *who is biggest?* is congruent with the coded information and the information asked for in the question *who is smallest?* is not. Although the RT for the incongruent question is 250 ms longer than for the congruent question, this difference is not significant: $t(651) = 1.21$, $p = 0.11$ one tail. It should be noted that for negative equative items the answer is always congruent with the coded information. This follows from the model described above. If the question is *who is biggest?*, the proposition in which A (the biggest boy) occurs is always coded as *A is bigger than B*. If the question is *who is smallest?*, the proposition that contains C (the smallest boy) is always coded as *C is smaller than B*.

What can be concluded so far with respect to the questions asked in Chap.2? The first conclusion concerns the coding of the information. The information of the comparatives is apparently coded semantically in unmarked form. There is no such uniform coding of the negative equatives. The code of the first proposition of the negative equatives depends on the adjective of the question. The second proposition is coded in such a way that the new term is the focus of the information, irrespective of the adjective.

The second conclusion concerns the complexity of the information. One can conclude that the more complex the information, the more the process is characterized by syntactic surface factors; the less complex the information, the more the process is characterized by semantic factors. The strategy in solving the comparative items seems to bypass part of the syntactic analysis. It is based on a more direct insight into the underlying meaning. That this strategy is not found for the negative equative items can be due to the higher mental load and the lack of external memory support in analyzing the negative equatives.

The third conclusion concerns the role of the question. Evidence is found for the fact that the more complex items, the negative equatives, are analyzed in function of the question and the less complex items, the comparatives, are not. It is clear that analysis in function of the question can reduce the complexity of the processing. Thus, the results illustrate the phenomenon discussed in the previous chapter that the more complex the information, the higher the premium on a strategy that reduces the cognitive strain.

Chapter 4   Storing the Information During a Time Interval

4.1 Experiment II

In this experiment the question is presented immediately after the two propositions. Two times are measured for each item: the inspection time, i.e.,
the time necessary to understand the propositions and the answering time,
i.e., the time necessary to answer the question.

What does the model predict with respect to the inspection times and the
answering times? It is a reasonable assumption that during the inspection
period the subject will analyze the propositions and integrate the information in the propositions. As the question is not yet presented, the boxes in
the model that refer to the question have to be deleted. The model for the
inspection times is presented in Fig. 4.1.

What about the answering times? According to the model the comparative
items are stored in unmarked form during the inspection period. Therefore,
it is expected that the RT for the congruent question *who is biggest?* will be
shorter than for the incongruent question *who is smallest?*.

The predictions for the negative equative items are somewhat different.
these three-term series are not stored in unmarked form during the inspection
period. The result of the inspection period is that the adjective of the firs
proposition is maintained, and that the second proposition is transformed
into either *A is bigger than B* or into *C is smaller than B*. It is unlikely,
however, that in the long run the information from the negative equative
items is stored in a different way than the information from the comparative
items. Accordingly, it is hypothesized that a similar process is going to
take place as for comparatives, namely that the propositions will be coded
in unmarked form. When enough time has elapsed, the negative equative items
will be stored in the same way as the comparative items. In Experiments III
and IV the time between the inspection of the propositions and the answering
of the question is increased, in order to determine in how much time the
ultimate coding is completed.

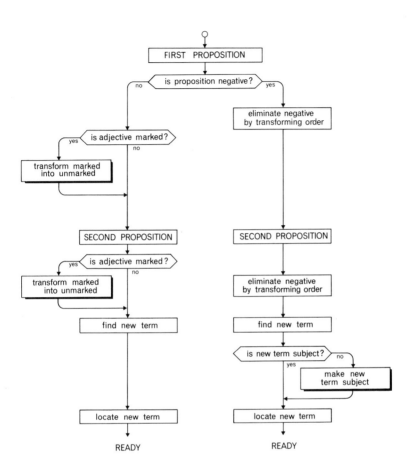

Fig. 4.1. Process model for the inspection times in Experiments II, III and IV

4.1.1 Method

The material was the same as in Experiment I. The subjects were 19 students
who volunteered in the experiment; they were paid for their participation.
No subject had participated in Experiment I.

The procedure was the same as in Experiment I, except for the following.
Three projectors have been used, one for the propositions, one for the question and the answer alternatives, and one for the blank inter-item interval.
The subject was instructed to try to understand the propositions and to com-
bine the information in the two propositions as quickly as possible. When he
had done so, he had to press a foot switch. The time was measured from the
onset of the presentation of the propositions until the moment the subject
pressed the foot switch. This time will be called the inspection time. When
the foot switch was pressed, the propositions disappeared and at the same
time the question and the answer alternatives were projected. The subject
had to give the answer by pressing one out of three response buttons, just
as in Experiment I. The time was measured from the onset of the presentation
of the question until the moment the subject pressed a response button. This
time will be called the answering time. The times were measured in ms.

4.1.2 Results and Discussion

It is only with respect to the answering time that one can establish whether
an item was solved incorrectly. When a subject had given a wrong answer the
item was considered as an error: the inspection time and the answering time
were both eliminated from the analysis.

The percentage of erroneous items averaged 5%. Subjects with more than
11 % errors were not included in the analysis. This resulted in the elimination of 5 out of 24 subjects.

Inspection times (RTi's). The data have been analyzed in the same way as
in Experiment I. Because the question does not differentiate the items at the
moment of the inspection of the propositions, there are 16 different item
types and six instances of each type. For each subject 16 medians have been
computed, one for each group of six similar items. These data have been analyzed by means of a one-way analysis of variance with repeated measures.
The means of these medians are presented in Table 4.1.

Predictions of the inspection data have been obtained in the following way
The process is considered to be the same as in the previous task, except,
of course, as far as the question is concerned. This yielded the model of
Fig. 4.1 as stated above. To each box that differentiates between the items

Table 4.1. Mean inspection times and answering times [ms] for the three-term series problems in Experiment II

		Form of propositions	Inspection time	Answering time Form of question biggest? smallest?	
I	a	A bigger than B; B bigger than C	6578	1676	1658
	b	B bigger than C; A bigger than B	6138	1578	1635
II	a	C smaller than B; B smaller than A	6698	1552	1740
	b	B smaller than A; C smaller than B	7469	1428	1575
III	a	A bigger than B; C smaller than B	6339	1669	1719
	b	C smaller than B; A bigger than B	5867	1530	1665
IV	a	B smaller than A; B bigger than C	6252	1577	1621
	b	B bigger than C; B smaller than A	6612	1627	1675
I'	a	A not as small as B; B not as small as C	8323	1830	1666
	b	B not as small as C; A not as small as B	8892	1633	1693
II'	a	C not as big as B; B not as big as A	7745	1436	1570
	b	B not as big as A; C not as big as B	8740	1570	1510
III'	a	A not as small as B; C not as big as B	8709	1735	1659
	b	C not as big as B; A not as small as B	8587	1457	1766
IV'	a	B not as big as A; B not as small as C	7411	1564	1721
	b	B not as small as C; B not as big as A	7578	1632	1786

the same numerical value was attributed as the value of the corresponding box in the previous model. In other words the parameter values are determined a priori, based on the previous experiment. By specifying which operations are involved in each item the RTi's can be predicted. The Pearson correlations between these predicted RTi's and the observed RTi's is 0.89. This correlation is 0.95 if the parameter values are determined, based on the data of the present experiment, as is specified below (see also Table 4.2).

The correspondence between the results (and the model) of Experiment I and the results of Experiment II has also been studied in detail. The comparisons between the means of Experiment I that can be made in this experiment have been computed. With the exception of one, all comparisons that were significant in Experiment I are also significant in this experiment, and no other than these. The RTi for negative equative items is 1754 ms longer than for comparative items $t(270) = 9.58$, $p < 0.001$. There is a marked-unmarked effect for comparative items, but not for negative equative items; the RTi for items with a marked adjective is longer than for items with an unmarked adjective;

Table 4.2. Summary of results of Experiment II

inspection times comparison	Difference [ms]
negative equative (NE) - comparative (Comp)	1754
marked - unmarked adjective first proposition Comp	155 n.s.
marked - unmarked adjective second proposition Comp	571
new term subject - point of reference NE	968

correlation with model r = 0.89
mean RTi 7371 ms

answering times comparison	Difference [ms]
marked - unmarked adjective first proposition NE	130
smallest? - *biggest?* for unmarked code	109

this difference is 571 ms for the adjective of the second proposition: $t(270) = 2.20$, $p < 0.05$. Contrary to the results of Experiment I, however, the marked-unmarked difference is not significant for the adjective of the first proposition. This is the only case in the four experiments that this difference is not significant. The difference was 155 ms in the predicted direction: $t(270) = 0.59$. The RTi is 968 ms longer when the new term in the second proposition of the negative equative items is subject than when it is the reference point: $t(270) = 3.73$, $p < 0.001$. The results are summarized in Table 4.2. These effects together account for 91% of the sum of squares between the items. The residual sum of squares is not significant: $F(12,270) = 0.92$. These differences are of the same order of magnitude as in Experiment I Only the difference between the negative equatives and the comparatives is somewhat larger; the time estimate of processing the negations is 1633 ms. This confirms the conclusion from Experiment I that in analyzing the negative equative items the question is anticipated which reduces the complexity of the processing of the negative equatives.

Answering times (RTa's). The answering data have been analyzed in the same way as the data in Experiment I. The same contrasts have been computed. The RTa for the negative equative items is not different from the RTa for the comparative items. Apparently, the negative propositions are stored as positive ones, which confirms the model. The fact that negative information, after a certain time interval, is transformed into and retained as positive information has also been observed by CARPENTER (1973). When the first proposition of the negative equative items was marked, the RTa is 130 ms longer than when the first proposition was unmarked: $t(558) = 3.11$, $p < 0.01$. This result indicates that in the answering period the relation between the first two terms is coded in unmarked form. This process is similar to the processing of the comparatives in Experiment I. This makes sense because the negation has been eliminated during the inspection period.

According to the model, the comparative items and one-half of the negative equative items (the items where A occurs in the second proposition) have been transformed in such a way that both the first and second proposition are coded in unmarked form. For these items the question *who is biggest?* was answered more quickly than the question *who is smallest?*, as was expected. This difference was 109 ms: $t(558) = 3.19$, $p < 0.01$. The other negative equatives, however (the items where C occurs in the second proposition), are not yet coded in a homogeneous unmarked form, according to the model. The first proposition is coded in unmarked form, the second one in marked form. For these items the RTa for the question *who is biggest?* did not in fact differ from the RTa for the question *who is smallest?* ($t = 0.60$); the RTa for the unmarked question was 36 ms longer than for the marked question. These results support the model: the comparatives are stored in unmarked form. In the course of time, the negative equatives tend to be coded in unmmarked form; the RTa for the question depends on the congruence of the question with the coded information: the unmarked question has an advantage over the marked question only when the information is coded in unmarked form. So the process for the answering time can be described by two operations. First, if the first adjective of a negative equative is marked, it is transformed into unmarked form. Second, if the adjective of the question does not match the adjective of the stored information, an adjective transformation takes place.

The proportion of the sum of squares between the items that is not accounted for by these two operations is not significant: $F < 1$.

The following conclusion can be drawn with respect to the transformation of the coded information over time. When there is only limited time available as in the task of Experiment I and in the inspection task of Experiment II, relatively complex information is coded in a temporary form which is good enough to determine the answer. When more time is available, the information tends to be coded in a more definite form, presumably a more basic form. This is what happened with the negative equative items during the answering period In the following experiments even more time is available to code the information.

4.2 Experiment III

This experiment is similar to the previous one. The only difference is that after the inspection period there is a blank interval of 4 s before the question and the answer alternatives are presented.

Based on the previous experiment, the following predictions are made. The inspection times must be very similar to those in Experiment II, because the two experiments differ only with respect to the interval after the inspection period. It should be noted, however, that in the inspection period a subject can anticipate the 4 s interval during which he can process the information.

The following predictions are made with respect to the answering times. In the previous experiments it was found that the comparatives are stored in unmarked form. The same is hypothesized for this experiment. Consequently, the only difference among the comparative items is whether the question is congruent with the stored information or not. This, again, is the marked-unmarked effect for the question.

It is supposed that the negative equatives are stored in unmarked form, just as the comparatives, when enough time is available. In the previous experiment it is found that during the answering period the first proposition is coded in unmarked form. It is hypothesized that after the 4 s time interval, the second proposition is also coded in unmarked form. Consequently, the same prediction is made for the negative equatives as for the comparatives: the RTa for the unmarked question which is congruent with the stored information is shorter than for the marked question.

4.2.1 Method

The material and the procedure were the same as in the previous experiment, except as far as the interval between the propositions and the question is concerned.

The subjects were 20 students who volunteered in the experiment. They were paid for their participation. None of these subjects had participated in any of the previous experiments.

4.2.2 Results and Discussion

Just as in Experiment II, an item was considered as an error if the answer to the question was wrong; both the inspection time and the answering time were then eliminated.

The percentage of errors averaged 4%. Because the number of errors of two subjects was very high (10 %) relative to the number of errors of the other 20 subjects, these two subjects were not included in the analysis.

Inspection times. The inspection data of this experiment are in agreement with those of Experiment II; the Pearson correlation between the two experiments is 0.90. The experiments differ, however, with respect to mean RTi: the mean RTi for 14 out of 16 items is shorter in Experiment III than in Experiment II. This difference is significant: sign test, $\chi^2(1) = 7.45$, $p < 0.01$. The items are on the average 532 ms shorter. This difference can be an effect of the time interval between the inspection and answering periods. During the inspection period subjects in Experiment III can anticipate the 4 s interval to process the information. Caution is required, however. If the two experiments are considered as two levels of one between subjects factor, the difference is not significant: $t(37) = 0.80$.

The data have been analyzed in the same way as in Experiment II. For each subject 16 medians for the correct responses have been computed, one for each group of six similar items. The means of these medians are presented in Table 4.3.

How well does the model account for the data? One can a priori predict the inspection times on the basis of the model using the parameters and the parameter values as obtained from Experiment I. Thus, these predictions are identical to those in Experiment II. The Pearson correlation between these predictions and the data is 0.92. This correlation is 0.94 if the parameter values are determined, in the way described earlier, on the basis of the data of the present experiment; these values, except for the processing of the negatives which was 978 ms, are presented in Table 4.4.

All the earlier mentioned comparisons between the means that apply to this experiment have been computed. Exactly the same factors have been found as

Table 4.3. Mean inspection times and answering times [ms] for the three-term series problems in Experiment III

		Form of propositions	Inspection time	Answering time Form of question biggest?	smallest?
I	a	A bigger than B; B bigger than C	5974	1758	1883
	b	B bigger than C; A bigger than B	5799	1642	1799
II	a	C smaller than B; B smaller than A	6515	1687	1919
	b	B smaller than A; C smaller than B	7006	1725	2004
III	a	A bigger than B; C smaller than B	5751	1822	1891
	b	C smaller than B; A bigger than B	6174	1734	2087
IV	a	B smaller than A; B bigger than C	6682	1577	1869
	b	B bigger than C; B smaller than A	5710	1719	1785
I'	a	A not as small as B; B not as small as C	7442	1766	1718
	b	B not as small as C; A not as small as B	8367	1690	2006
II'	a	C not as big as B; B not as big as A	6997	1552	1679
	b	B not as big as A; C not as big as B	8333	1748	1862
III'	a	A not as small as B; C not as big as B	8179	1818	1753
	b	C not as big as B; A not as small as B	7960	1524	1923
IV'	a	B not as big as A; B not as small as C	6209	1649	1980
	b	B not as small as C; B not as big as A	6318	1641	1850

in Experiments I and II; there was only a difference with respect to the marked-unmarked results for the comparatives. The RTi for negative equative items is 1274 ms longer than for comparative items: $t(285) = 8.40$, $p < 0.001$. Again, there is a marked-unmarked effect for comparative items, and not for negative equative items: the RTi for items with a marked adjective is longer than for items with an unmarked adjective; this difference is 786 ms for the adjective of the first proposition: $t(285) = 3.68$, $p < 0.001$. Contrary to the results of Experiments I and II, however, the marked-unmarked difference is not significant for the adjective of the second proposition; the difference was 88ms: $t(285) = 0.41$. The RTi is 1468 ms longer when the new term in the second proposition of the negative equative items is subject than when it is the reference point: $t(285) = 6.87$, $p < 0.001$. These contrasts account for 89% of the sum of squares between items. The remaining sum of squares is not significant: $F(12,285) = 1.39$, $0.10 < p < 0.25$. The results are summarized in Table 4.4.

Table 4.4. Summary of results of Experiment III

inspection times comparison	Difference [ms]
negative equative (NE) - comparative (Comp)	1274
marked - unmarked adjective first proposition Comp	786
marked - unmarked adjective second proposition Comp	88 n.s.
new term subject - point of reference NE	1468

correlation with model r = 0.92
mean RTi 6838 ms

answering times comparison	Difference [ms]
smallest? - *biggest?* Comp	197
smallest? - *biggest?* NE	173
reduction of *smallest?* - *biggest?* by availability NE	90

The absence of the marked-unmarked difference for the second proposition could be explained by assuming that the second proposition is temporarily stored and not processed until the interval. Accordingly, the RTi for items with the marked adjective in the second proposition in Experiment II was greater (525 ms) than the RTi of the same items in Experiment III, whereas the RTi for the items with the unmarked adjective in the second proposition was indeed approximately equal in the two experiments, the difference being only 51 ms.

Answering times. As was predicted, the only difference among the comparative items is whether the question is marked or unmarked. This difference is 197 ms: $t(589) = 4.80$, $p < 0.001$. The same result is found for the negative equative items, the difference being 173 ms: $t(589) = 4.22$, $p < 0.001$. So, during the time interval, the information is apparently coded in unmarked form. The process in the answering time can then be described in terms of a congruence effect as in the previous experiment: if the adjective of the question does not match the adjective of the stored information, an adjective transformation takes place.

One other effect has been found for the negative equatives. The difference in RTa between the question *who is smallest?* and *who is biggest?* is 90 ms greater $[t(589) = 2.19, p < 0.05]$ for items in which the adjective of the second proposition was unmarked after the transformations in the inspection period than for the items in which the adjective of the second proposition was marked after the transformations in the inspection period. This can be explained as follows. During the interval the second proposition when marked (*C is smaller than B*) is transformed into unmarked form. The new term in this second proposition is more available than the old term, because the new term has just been operated upon. That new term is always the answer to the question *who is smallest?* Consequently, the availability or recency effect reduces the RTa for the question *who is smallest?*. Similar recency effects have been found in Experiment I which are represented by the last operation in the model. Parenthetically, the proportion of the sum of squares between the items that is not accounted for by the two effects that are just described is not significant: $F(29,589) = 1.40$, $p > 0.05$.

One may conclude that the processes during the answering period in which, according to the model, the negations are eliminated already, are very similar to the processes with the comparative items in Experiment I.

This experiment confirms the conclusions of the earlier experiments with respect to the problem of how information is coded and transformed over time. The information in the three-term series problems is in the end stored in unmarked form. There is an interaction process between complexity of the information and the time available to process the information. Less complex information, like the comparatives, is relatively soon transformed and coded in unmarked form. The more complex the information, the more time is needed to transform it into the final format. There is a gradual process of these transformations. Under high time pressure (Experiment I) there is no evidence

that the complex information is coded in unmarked form. The reasoning process is determined by syntactic factors. Under relatively low time pressure
(Experiment II), the first proposition is transformed into the unmarked form;
this is done during the answering period. It is only when still more time is
available (the time interval of Experiment III) that also the second proposition is coded in unmarked form. These conclusions will be tested again in
the following experiment in which the time interval is even longer. It is expected that the effect of the order of the propositions that still was found
in the answering period of Experiment III will disappear in the following
experiment, because of the longer time interval.

4.3 Experiment IV

This experiment is similar to the previous one. The only difference is that
the time interval between the inspection period and the answering period was
8 s.

The predictions with respect to the inspection times are the same as in
Experiments II and III. With respect to the answering times it is expected
again that the RTa for the items with the unmarked question will be shorter
than for the items with the marked question, because the information is
stored in unmarked form. In the previous experiment it was found that the
RTa difference between the marked and the unmarked question for the negative
equative items was smaller when the smallest term occurred in the second proposition than when it occurred in the first proposition. This effect was attributed to the greater availability of the smallest term after a marked-
unmarked transformation in the former case. It is supposed that this effect
will disappear in the present experiment: when the time interval after that
transformation increases, the difference in availability will disappear.

4.3.1 Method

The material and the procedure were the same as in the previous experiments.
The subjects were 20 students who volunteered in the experiment. They were
paid for their participation. None of these subjects had participated in any
of the previous experiments.

4.3.2 Results and Discussion

The data have been analyzed in the same way as in the previous experiment.
The percentage of errors was on the average 2.5%. Subjects with more than 6%

errors were not included in the analysis. This resulted in the elimination of 3 out of 23 subjects.

Inspection times. The Pearson correlation with the inspection data of Experiment II is 0.87; the correlation with Experiment III is 0.91. The mean RTi is again shorter than in Experiment II, the difference being 628 ms. The mean RTi for 15 out of 16 items is shorter than in Experiment II. This difference is significant: sign test, $\chi^2(1) = 10.56$, $p < 0.01$, and can be attributed to the anticipation of the time interval between the inspection and the answering periods. This result is in complete agreement with Experiment III.

Table 4.5. Mean inspection times and answering times [ms] for the three-term series problems in Experiment IV

		Form of propositions	Inspection time	Answering time Form of question biggest? smallest?	
I	a	A bigger than B; B bigger than C	5754	1821	1923
	b	B bigger than C; A bigger than B	4935	1731	1908
II	a	C smaller than B; B smaller than A	5906	1714	1798
	b	B smaller than A; C smaller than B	6708	2014	2102
III	a	A bigger than B; C smaller than B	5518	1920	1896
	b	C smaller than B; A bigger than B	5760	1744	1884
IV	a	B smaller than A; B bigger than C	6988	1609	1994
	b	B bigger than C; B smaller than A	6196	1692	1891
I'	a	A not as small as B; B not as small as C	7657	1677	1880
	b	B not as small as C; A not as small as B	8781	1787	1822
II'	a	C not as big as B; B not as big as A	6643	1708	1826
	b	B not as big as A; C not as big as B	7422	2127	2118
III'	a	A not as small as B; C not as big as B	8381	2134	2062
	b	C not as big as B; A not as small as B	8334	1699	1998
IV'	a	B not as big as A; B not as small as C	6850	1620	2178
	b	B not as small as C; B not as big as A	6064	1730	2017

For each subject 16 medians for the correct responses have been computed. The means of these medians are represented in Table 4.5. The Pearson correlation of these means with the a priori predictions based on the model is 0.87. This correlation is 0.89 if the parameter values are determined based on the

data of the present experiment; these values, except for the processing of
the negatives which is 1315 ms, are specified below.

The effects that had been found in Experiment III were found again in
this experiment. The RTi for negative equative items is 1546 ms longer than
for comparative items: $t(285) = 7.93$, $p < 0.001$. There is a marked-unmarked
effect for comparative items: the RTi for items with a marked adjective is
longer than for items with an unmarked adjective; this difference is 740 ms
for the adjective of the first proposition: $t(285) = 2.68$, $p < 0.01$. Again
this effect is not significant for the adjective of the second proposition;
the difference was 223 ms in the predicted direction: $t(285) = 0.81$. The RTi
is 1426 ms longer when the new term in the second proposition of the negative equative items is subject than when it is the reference point: $t(285) =$
5.17, $p < 0.001$. These contrasts account for 78% of the sum of squares between items. These results are summarized in Table 4.6.

The absence of the marked-unmarked difference for the second proposition
of the comparative items confirms the result of Experiment III; that proposition is not processed until the interval. Accordingly, the RTi for items
with the marked adjective in the second proposition in Experiment II was again
longer (697 ms) than the RTi for the same items in Experiment IV, whereas the
RTi difference between the two experiments for the items with the unmarked
adjective in the second proposition was much smaller, only 349 ms.

The predicted effects account for only 78% of the sum of squares between
the items. Several other effects should be mentioned. For homogeneous negative equative items it is found that the RTi for marked items is 1187 ms
longer than for unmarked items: $t(285) = 3.04$, $p < 0.01$. This effect would
not in any way be in conflict with the present theory of coding information
in unmarked form. Another effect concerns the comparative items: the RTi
for incongruent items (Table 4.5, items IV) is 953 ms longer than for congruent items (items III): $t(285) = 2.44$, $p < 0.05$. It should be noted, however, that if these a posteriori comparisons are tested with an a posteriori
testing procedure, the effects are not significant (SCHEFFE, $p > 0.25$). Never-
theless the latter contrast deserves some attention because other authors did
find this difference (CLARK, 1969a; POTTS and SCHOLZ, 1975). This contrast
can be interpreted as a reference point-subject effect, completely in agreement with the results of the negative equative items: the RTi is shorter if
the new term is subject than when it is the reference point. This effect,
however, appears to depend on the adjective in the second proposition. It
only occurs if the second adjective is unmarked, the difference being 1024 ms,
but not if the second adjective is marked, the difference being 62 ms in the

50

Table 4.6. Summary of results of Experiment IV

inspection times comparison	Difference [ms]
negative equative (NE) - comparative (Comp)	1546
marked - unmarked adjective first proposition Comp	740
marked - unmarked adjective second proposition Comp	223 n.s.
new term subject - point of reference NE	1426
marked - unmarked for homogeneous NE	1186
incongruent - congruent Comp	953

correlation with model $r = 0.87$
mean RTi 6743 ms

answering times comparison	Difference [ms]
smallest? - *biggest?* Comp	144
smallest? - *biggest?* NE	177

opposite direction. A rather speculative explanation might be that the processing of the second proposition of the comparative items consists in two optional operations: the marked-unmarked transformation is preceded by a transformation in which the new term is made the subject of the proposition. The proposition *B is bigger than C* has to undergo both transformations, while the proposition *A is bigger than B* does not have to undergo any transformation; *B is smaller than A* must undergo only the former transformation, and *C i smaller than B* must undergo only the latter transformation. Accordingly, the

reference point-subject effect should be much smaller for the items with
the marked adjective, if it exists at all, than for items with the unmarked
adjective in the second proposition. This explanation could account for the
lack of difference between items with the marked and unmarked adjective in
the second proposition. However, the reference point-subject effect for
items with unmarked adjective in the second proposition is an a posteriori
effect and it was not found in the previous experiments. Consequently, the
earlier explanation, that the adjective of the second proposition is not
processed until the interval, is preferred.

  Answering times. As was predicted, the RTa for the question *who is smallest?*
was longer than for the question *who is biggest?*; for the comparative items
the difference was 144 ms: $t(589) = 2.45$, $p < 0.05$; and for the negative
equative items 177 ms: $t (589) = 3.02$, $p < 0.01$. The process during the answering period can be described in terms of a congruence effect, just as in
the previous experiments: if the adjective of the question does not match the
adjective of the stored information, an adjective transformation takes place.
The proportion of the sum of squares between the items that is not accounted
for by this effect is indeed not significant: $F(30,589) = 1.46$, $p > 0.05$.

  Furthermore, the RTa difference between the marked and unmarked question
for the negative equative items in which the smallest term occurred in the
second proposition was not smaller than the RTa difference for the items in
which the largest term occurred in the second proposition. This again is
what was expected; the difference was only 7 ms. In the previous experiments
it had been observed that in fact the information processed most recently
is most available. The last operation found for the negative equative items
in the previous experiment was the marked-unmarked transformation for the
second proposition (*C is smaller than B*), which increased the availability
of *C*. The availability was inherent to the order of processing the information and, consequently, to the order of the propositons. Therefore it should
disappear once the information is stored in the definite form. This experiment confirms furthermore the conclusions of the previous experiments: the
definite form in which the information is coded is the unmarked form.

  The results with respect to the transformation of information have also been found by other authors. KINTSCH and MONK (1972) found that, when a
text had been coded, there was no differential difficulty in making inferences from the text, whether the presented text was syntactically complex or
simple. Memory representation is a conceptual rather than a linguistic structure. A similar result has been obtained by KING and GREENO (1974) for arith-
metic problems. The decreasing importance of the coding of the surface form

of a sentence has been illustrated by studies of KEENAN and KINTSCH (1974) and by McKOON and KEENAN (1974). These studies demonstrated a weakening of the surface form of the sentence for a 20 min time delay, while memory for meaning remained intact. GARROD and TRABASSO (1973) found a syntactic congruity effect between a question and the sentence the question was about, but only when that sentence immediately preceded the question. The surface coding is transformed into a propositional coding. Similarly, ANDERSON (1974) demonstrated that after a time delay an abstract propositional representation of a sentence comes to dominate a verbatim representation.

Chapter 5   Solving Pictorial Problems

The following two experiments deal with three-term series problems composed
not of verbal statements but of simple drawings of line segments of different slope. The aim of these experiments is to investigate the extent to which
reasoning processes with verbal material are similar to reasoning processes
with pictorial material. At the same time these experiments provide more evidence on the way in which verbal and pictorial information is coded in memory.

5.1 Experiment V

The question to be answered now is: To what extent does the model for reasoning with verbal three-term series problems generalize to comparable nonverbal problems? This question refers specifically to the nature of the processes by which one combines the pieces of information of the two premises
in order to construct the three-term series and to obtain the answer. According to the model, the relation between the two terms of the first proposition is coded. Then the new term is located with respect to the old
terms. The RT is shorter if the answer to the question is the term that has
just been located. Parenthetically, it should be noted that the use of the
word "locate" reminds one of the processes of the imagery hypothesis of
HUTTENLOCHER; however, no attempt will be made here to investigate whether
the processes with verbal material are analogous to the determination of the
location of an object in a physical array. The point is that the processes
of combining the information from the two propositions and of obtaining the
answer are described in the model in a way that is neutral with respect to
the verbal or pictorial properties of the material. The question then arises
as to whether those processes apply to pictorial material as well as to verbal material.

The other question refers to the coding of the information. In the description of the processes given above, it is claimed that the information is
finally coded in unmarked form. In the present and the following experiments,

material is used that is hard to verbalize: it consists of line segments of different slope. The question is whether the coding of the information, and as a consequence the retrieval processes, during the answering period are different from those in the previous experiment.

The task in these experiments was comparable to the reasoning task of the previous experiments. Because the aim of the experiments was to compare the processing of verbal and pictorial information, pictures have been selected which could not easily be coded verbally. The material consisted of three-term series in which the terms were line segments of different slope. The construction the subject had to make was a vertical arrangement of the three line segments. The question to be answered was: which line segment is the highest (lowest) in that arrangement? The experimental procedure was comparable, but not identical, to the one used in the previous experiments. The information on the construction of the three-term series was not given at once; it was given in two steps (Fig. 5.1). First, the relation between two line segments was given; then, the relation between one of these line segments and the new one. The reason was that this procedure would presumably decrease the likelihood that subjects adopt a very task specific strategy, based, e.g., on a directly matching of the one identical line segment. The time necessary for the construction of the three-term series was measurd (inspection time).

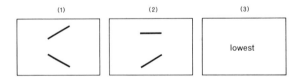

Fig. 5.1. Example of an item of Experiment V

Then, the question was presented and the time necessary for the production of the answer was measured (answering time). This procedure is comparable to the one used in the verbal three-term series problems.

If the pictures are scanned and coded from top to bottom as CLARK and CHASE (1972) suggest, one can expect that the order of presentation 2-1 (see Fig. 5.1) is easier than 1-2. In the first case the three-term is constructed throughout from top to bottom; even the combination of the two pictures is made from top to bottom. In the second case the combination of the

pictures is made from bottom to top, the exact opposite to the coding of
the pictures. For similar observations, see JONES (1970). This prediction
is very similar to HUNTER's idea of natural order in reasoning (1957). This
prediction concerns the inspection times; the following prediction refers to
the answering times. It is expected that the RTa for the question *highest?*
will not differ from the RTa for the question *lowest?*. In the previous experiments the difference between the question *who is smallest?* and *who is biggest?*
was attributed to the (in)congruence between the question and the coding of
the required information; it was not an effect of marking per se. In all cases
where the information of the propositions was coded in unmarked form, the
RTa for the unmarked question was shorter than for the marked question
(answering times of Experiments III and IV both for comparative and negative
items; answering times of Experiment II for comparative items and one-half
of the negative equative items; for the comparative items in Experiment I
this difference was 250 ms, but not significant). On the other hand, in all
cases in which the information was not yet coded in unmarked form, the RTa
for the unmarked question did not differ from the RTa for the marked question
(the negative equative items in Experiment I, the answering times of the
other half of the negative equative items in Experiment II). Consequently, in
the present experiment, where the pictures are not supposed to be coded in
a verbal form, there is no congruence at all between the question and the
coded information. Accordingly, the RTa difference between the answer for the
marked question and the answer for the unmarked question should disappear.

One thing, however, has to be explained with respect to the marked-unmarked
effect in the previous experiments. It has been concluded that the information is coded in unmarked form. Presumably, the unmarked form is more basic
than the marked form. But then the question arises why there is no difference between the marked and unmarked adjective of the question. In other
words, it must be explained how the asymmetry between marked and unmarked
concepts can disappear. In NOORDMAN (1978) marked and unmarked concepts are
assumed to differ with respect to the foreground quality of the contrasting
feature. Consequently, if that feature is stressed, that difference should
disappear. This was indeed observed. This point will be discussed later on.

5.1.1 Method

Material. One of the line segments was horizontal; the other two segments
made an angle of 35 deg clockwise and 35 deg counterclockwise with the horizontal. With the three line segments, six different three-term series can
be constructed. The first presentation can be the top pair or the bottom

pair; the question can be *highest?* or *lowest?*. Thus, there are four different items for each three-term series. This makes a total of 24 items. There were two blocks of experimental items; the first item in each block was a practice item. The different three-term series underlying each item and the different item types (top vs bottom pair first; question *highest?* vs *lowest?*) were evenly distributed among the blocks and within the blocks. A particular three-term series did not occur more than once in three consecutive items. Two consecutive items were always of a different type. Not more than three consecutive items required the same answer. Not more than two consecutive items contained the same question. The second pair of line segments in an item was never the same as the first pair of line segments in the following item. Each one of the three different line segments was the correct answer in each block an equal number of times. There were 12 practice items. The same restrictions held true for the construction and for the order of presentation of these items as for the experimental items. These practice items, except for the one that occurred in each experimental block, were grouped in one practice block preceding the experimental items.

Subjects. Eighteen university students served as subjects. They volunteered in the experiment; they were paid for their participation.

Procedure. The same equipment as in the previous experiments has been used. A pair of line segments subtended a visual angle of about 7 deg in the horizontal direction and a visual angle of about 11 deg in the vertical direction. The first pair of line segments was presented with a slide projector for 5 s. Then the second pair was presented. The subject was instructed to integrate the two pairs of line segments so as to construct a single configuration of the three line segments. He had to do this as quickly as possible. The time was measured from the onset of the presentation of the second pair until the subject pressed a foot switch to indicate that he had combined the two pairs of line segments. This time is again called the inspection time. Immediately after the inspection period, the question (*highest?* or *lowest?*) was presented. The subject had to decide which line segment was the highest one or lowest one in the configuration of the three line segments. He had to give the answer by pressing the button that corresponded to that line segment. There were three buttons that had a one-to-one correspondence with the three line segments; each button was labeled with a line segment. Because each one of the three different line segments was the correct answer in each block an equal number of times, the response buttons were balanced with respect to the correct answer. The time was measured from the onset of the presentation of the question until the answer was given. This time is again called the an-

swering time. The answering period was followed by a blank interval of 4 s.
The experiment lasted about 25 min.

5.1.2 Results

Subjects with more than four errors, i.e., 16%, were not included in the analysis. This resulted in the elimination of six subjects. The mean number of
errors for the remaining 18 subjects was 1.4, i.e., 6%.

Inspection times. Because the question does not differentiate among the
items as presented during the inspection period, there are only two item
types - the upper pair or the lower pair being presented first - with twelve
items for each type; two for each three-term series. For each subject, the
median of each item type has been computed for the correct responses. The mean
of the medians of the items in which the top pair is presented first is 3901
ms; the mean for the items in which the bottom pair is presented first is
4280 ms. This difference, tested with a one-way analysis of variance with
repeated measured, is not significant: $F(1,17) = 1.56$, $0.10 < p < 0.25$.

Answering times. For each subject four medians for the correct answers
have been computed, one for each item type: upper pair first or lower pair
first, combined with the question *highest?* or *lowest?*. The means of the medians are presented in Table 5.1. There is no difference between the items with

Table 5.1. Mean answering times [ms] for the pictorial three-term series
problems in Experiment V

Order of presentation	Form of question	
	biggest?	smallest?
upper pair first	1428	1325
lower pair first	1257	1651

the question *highest?* and *lowest?*: $F(1,51) = 3.31$, $p > 0.05$. There is no difference between the items in which the top pair is presented first or second:
$F(1,51) = 0.93$. Only the interaction is significant: $F(1,51) = 9.58$, $p < 0.01$.
This means that the RTa is shorter when the answer is a line segment of the
second pair than when it is a line segment of the first pair.

5.1.3 Discussion

The finding that the inspection time for the items in which the upper pair
is presented first was not significantly shorter than for the items in which

the lower pair is presented first can be explained in one of two ways. First, there is no preference at all to process a picture from top to bottom. In the light of other studies (CLARK and CHASE, 1972; VAN DEN BOS, 1974) this conclusion does not seem very plausible. The alternative conclusion is that the two pairs of line segments are not integrated into one three-term series during the inspection period. This conclusion is supported by the findings of the answering times. There is an interaction between the order of presentation of the pairs with the question. When the construction is made from top to bottom, the RT for the question about the bottom is shorter than for the question about the top. The reverse is found when the construction is made from bottom to top. This is the recency effect found in the previous experiments: if the answer is the term that has just been located with respect to the old terms, the RT is shorter than when the answer is one of the old terms. That this recency effect occurs in the answering period suggests that the three-term series is not constructed during the inspection time. The integration of the information does not take place until the answering period.

The results so far show that the processes of combining and integrating the information from the two pairs of line segments bear a close resemblance to the processes of combining and integrating the information from the two propositions in the earlier experiments. First, the three-term series is not constructed in a preferred way from top to bottom as one would expect on the basis of the image theories of DE SOTO et al. and of HUTTENLOCHER. This was not found for the verbal three-term series, either. Second, some of the information that is presented in the inspection period is not processed in the inspection period but only at the moment the question is presented. In this experiment, the integration of the two pairs of lines is made during the answering period. In the experiments on verbal three-term series, part of the coding process takes place during the answering period. Third, the recency effect is found again. In solving three-term series, the relation between the first two terms is determined, and afterwards the third term is located with respect to these two terms: the third term is more available than the other terms. Consequently, it may be concluded that the model of the solution of three-term series applies to the processing of pictorial information as well as to verbal information. This is true for processes of integrating the information only and not for the coding of the information. The pictorial and verbal information are coded in different ways. No difference in RT is found between the question *highest?* and *lowest?*. If the information of the pictures were coded in unmarked form, as was the case with the verbal problems, the RT for the question *highest?* would have to be shorter than for the question

lowest? because of the congruence between the question and the stored information. This is exactly what was found with the verbal three-term series
problems. The absence of this effect in the present experiment means that
the information is not coded in a verbal way. At the same time, this absence
confirms the interpretation of the difference between the marked and the unmarked question in the previous experiments: this difference was not attributed to the greater complexity of the marked adjective per se, but to the
congruence between question and stored information. Otherwise the same difference would have to have appeared in the present experiment as well.

5.2 Experiment VI

This experiment deals with the same questions as the previous one; but more
specifically it is concerned with the third problem investigated in the present study: To what extent is the reasoning process determined by the question? Therefore, the question is now presented before the two pairs of line
segments. Consequently, the information can be processed in relation to the
question; this was not possible in the previous experiment. It is clear that
the difference between Experiments VI and V to a large extent parallels the
difference between Experiments I and II.

5.2.1. Method

The same material has been used as in the previous experiment. Twenty-one
university students served as subjects. They volunteered in the experiment;
they were paid for their participation.

The question was presented for 2 s. Immediately after the question, the
first pair of line segments was presented for 5 s, followed by the second
pair of line segments. The RT was measured from the onset of the presentation of the second pair, until the subject pressed a button to give his answer. In all other respects, the procedure was the same as in Experiment V.

5.2.2 Results

Subjects with more than four errors, i.e., 16%, were not included in the
analysis. This resulted in the elimination of six subjects. The mean number
of errors for the remaining 21 subjects was 1.3, i.e., 5%.

There were four item types, just as for the answering times in Experiment V.
For each subject, four medians have been computed for the item types. The means
of the medians are represented in Table 5.2. There is no difference between

Table 5.2. Mean latencies [ms] for the pictorial three-term series problems in Experiment VI (question first)

Order of presentation	Form of question	
	biggest?	smallest?
upper pair first	2818	3443
lower pair first	3697	3050

the items with the question *highest?* and *lowest?*: $F(1,60) = 0.00$; nor between the items in which the top pair is presented first or second: $F(1,60) = 1.91$, $0.10 < p < 0.25$. The interaction is significant: $F(1,60) = 13.09$, $p < 0.001$. The interaction, however, is just the reverse of the interaction in the previous experiment: the RT is shorter when the answer is a line segment of the first pair than when it is a line segment of the second pair.

5.2.3 Discussion

The absence of the two main effects confirms the conclusions of the previous experiment. First, not surprisingly, the pictorial problems are not coded in unmarked form. Second, there is no preference to construct the three-term series from top to bottom. The interaction effect can be explained in two ways. In the first interpretation, the results differ only superficially from those of Experiment V. Subjects integrate the two pairs of the segments, as they are instructed to do, at the moment the second pair is presented. The easiest way, then, is to insert the first pair into the second pair and not the other way around. The reason is that at that moment the second pair is being presented to them. The second pair is then treated as the fixed pair or as the given information, and the first pair is the new information that has to be related to the given information. If the answer is found in the new pair, the RT is shorter than if the answer is found in the given or fixed pair. Interpreted in this way, the interaction effect is exactly the recency effect found in the previous experiment as well as in the experiments with verbal three-term series problems.

   The other interpretation of the interaction effect is more straight-forward, but it rests on the assumption that the subjects, contrary to instruction, do not integrate the two pairs of line segments. When the first pair of line segments is presented, the subjects retain as a provisional answer that line segment which is the highest or lowest of the pair depending on whether the question was *highest?* or *lowest?*, respectively. If that

line segment does not occur in the second pair, it is the definitive answer.
If it does occur in the second pair, that pair has to be examined more close-
ly, because the other line segment of that pair is the definitive answer.
This increases the RT. In this interpretation, the information is processed
in the chronological order of presentation.

The introspective reports of the subjects suggest that both strategies
have been used. Ten out of the twenty-one subjects reported that they had integrated the two pairs of line segments. Eight subjects reported that they
had not integrated the two pairs of line segments, and that they had used
the second strategy, to be called the "provisional" strategy. Three subjects
reported to have used none or both of these strategies; their results have not
been included in the following analysis. The RTs for each of the groups ex-
hibited the same pattern, as they should. The groups did differ with respect
to the mean RT: the mean RT for the subjects who had integrated the two pairs
was 4200 ms; the mean RT for the subjects who reported the provisional strategy was 2175 ms. The provisional strategy is the most economic of the two,
because less information has to be processed. Thus, the difference in RT confirms that the two groups differed with respect to the strategy they used.
Each one of the strategies produces the interaction effect.

Conclusion

In the present study a model has been developed for the reasoning process with three-term series problems. The information in the three-term series is finally coded in unmarked form. That form is established gradually, depending on the syntactic complexity of the item. The comparative items are coded immediately in unmarked form. Syntactically more complex information, such as negative equative items, is not coded in unmarked form under high time stress. The processes are determined by syntactic surface factors such as the grammatical function of the new term. When more time is available, the information tends to be coded in unmarked form. The transformations into the unmarked form occur in the sequential order of the presentation of the information. With less time stress, the first proposition is coded in unmarked form. When still more time is available to process the information, the second proposition is also coded in unmarked form.

The sequential order of the processing of the information is also illustrated by the recency effect. Not all information is equally available. The difference in availability can be explained in terms of order of processing: that information is most available which has just been processed (see also CARPENTER, 1973).

One can reduce the complexity of the processing by analyzing the information as it relates to the question. This procedure is adopted in the analysis of the more complex information, the negative equative items.

The processing of pictorial three-term series problems appears to be very similar to the processing of verbal three-term series problems. In both cases, no preferred top-down direction of processing has been observed. In both cases evidence has been found that the three-term series is not constructed until the moment the question is asked, although this construction could be made at an earlier moment. Moreover, the recency effect has been found in both cases: the most recently processed information is more available than earlier processed information.

The pictorial and verbal three-term series differ with respect to the coding of the information. The pictorial three-term series is not coded in unmarked form. Evidence for this conclusion is the absence of the marked-unmarked effect of the question. This absence confirms that the marked-unmarked effect of the question in verbal three-term series problems is due to the congruence of the question with the stored information and not to the marking of the question per se. Two remarks should be made with respect to the marked-unmarked effect of the question in verbal three-term series problems. First, one might claim that the verbal three-term series tends to be coded as an imagery ordering of the three terms, e.g., in a vertical dimension. That ordering would be established gradually in the course of time, as has been similarly claimed for the gradual coding in unmarked form. Postulating that a subject, in answering the question, scans that image in a top-down direction, one can account for the fact that the RT for the question *who is biggest?* is shorter than for the question *who is smallest?*. If, however, the information is coded in an imagery ordering which is scanned in a top-down direction, the results for the verbal and pictorial three-term series problems should be similar. But in the case of the pictorial problems no difference is found between the RT for the question *highest?* and *lowest?*.

The second remark to be made refers to the question raised earlier: if the information of the three-term series problems is coded in unmarked form because it is more basic, why is there no marked-unmarked effect of the question per se? It has been established, especially by CLARK (1974), that generally the unmarked form is cognitively less complex than the marked form. This difference can be attributed to the fact that an unmarked term can be used in a noncontrastive sense. In NOORDMAN (1978) it is proposed that the difference between contrastive and noncontrastive sense of marked-unmarked word pairs is a difference in the foreground quality of the feature on which the words differ. In the noncontrastive sense of the unmarked word, that feature is more background information than in the contrastive sense of the marked and unmarked words. It is assumed that background information is taken for granted more easily than foreground information, because it is not explicitly communicated.

However, if the feature on which the contrastive and the noncontrastive senses differ is stressed, that feature becomes relatively foreground information. Consequently, the asymmetry between the marked and the unmarked words should disappear: the unmarked word is used in the contrastive sense, just as the marked word. This is what happened in the present experiments. The question *highest?* specifies the positive pole on the vertical dimension and the question *lowest?*, the negative pole. The subject has to make a decision on this polarity. Thus, the positive and the negative poles are equally stressed; the feature + polar is equally foreground information as the feature - polar. The concepts *highest* and *lowest* will be symmetrical concepts in those tasks and no difference in RT is to be expected for the comprehension of these concepts.

This argument must also apply to the verbal three-term series problems, though: *biggest* and *smallest* are equally stressed; they require an equal processing load. But in these experiments a difference in RT is found between the unmarked and the marked question. That difference, however, is not attributed to the coding of the concepts *biggest* and *smallest* per se. It was explained in terms of congruence between the question and the coding of the required information. The difference in RT between the marked and unmarked question is evidence for the fact that the verbal three-term series are coded in unmarked form. The absence of this effect for the pictorial three-term series indicates that there is no such congruence between the question and the coding of the required information. The pictorial three-term series is not coded in the same format as the verbal three-term series.

Part II Processing Conditional Relations

The aim of this part is to characterize the psychological processing of a
conditional relation. Conditional relations are studied in the form of sentences with different conditional conjunctions. Several experimental ways
have been used to approach this goal. The part consists of three chapters.

In the first chapter the meaning of conditional sentences has been studied.
The results of a reasoning experiment demonstrated the extent to which the
interpretation of a conditional sentence depends on the meaning a subject
attributes to the conjunction and to what extent it depends on the knowledge
of the facts expressed in the propositions. It appeared that the conditional
conjunctions are interpreted predominantly as expressions of an equivalence
relation, even if this is in conflict with the knowledge of the facts expressed in the propositions. There were, however, some differences between
the conjunctions in this respect. In another experiment the meaning of a conditional sentence was approached in a rather direct way. Subjects had to judge conditional sentences with respect to the similarity of meaning. A difference in the nature of the communication in conditional sentences was demonstrated viz. between sentences expressing a condition-consequence relation
and sentences expressing an inference relation.

The second chapter concerns the question of how a conditional sentence is
stored in memory and reproduced. The results of a memory experiment indicated
that the conjunction *if* ... *then* is a very basic conjunction in the sense
that conditional relations tend to be reproduced in *if* ... *then* form.

The third chapter deals with the understanding of conditional sentences
from an information processing point of view. Time estimates are obtained
for the factors that appeared important in the previous experiments, and a
description is given of the processes of understanding conditional sentences.

Introduction

Whatever the process of understanding may be, when information is understood, it must be assimilated to cognitive categories, structures, or programs. The nature of these structures is at present a widely studied topic in psychology, as witness the amount of work in the fields of semantic memory and artificial intelligence of natural language. Most of the experimental work has dealt with structures and processing of concepts underlying nouns, and with relations between these concepts. For some overview articles see SMITH et al. (1974); COLLINS and LOFTUS (1975); BREUKER (1976); NOORDMAN-VONK and NOORDMAN (1975) and SMITH (1978), NOORDMAN-VONK (1979).

The present study deals with relational concepts; more specifically with conditional relations. The aim is to characterize the conceptual representation of a conditional relation. Several ways will be used to approach this goal. It will be investigated as to how a conditional relation is interpreted how a conditional relation is coded in memory, and how the processing of such a relation must be characterized.

Natural language has available several conditional conjunctions to express a conditional relation in the format of a sentence. A question which arises in whether the conjunctions differ in cognitive complexity in the sense that a conditional relation is more easily expressed and understood in the form of one conjunction rather than in another.

One reminder should be given. Very different messages can be expressed in conditional sentences. A conditional sentence may have the specific meaning of a warning, a promise, a threat; it may express a causal or temporal relation, a definition, or still some other specific relation. In fact, the meaning of a conditional sentence depends on the content of the propositions and on the larger context of the sentence. Any account of conditional sentences in terms of abstract propositions will be insufficient. Recently, FILLENBAUM (1974, 1975, 1976) has studied conditional sentences that varied in meaning, depending on such contextual factors. It is unlikely that the different conditional relations correspond to one underlying conceptual representation. In the present study a restriction is made in the kinds of conditional sentences to be studied. No sentences are used where the speaker and the listener are primarily involved as persons trying to influence the behavior of one another as is the case in, e.g., threats, warnings, promises.

As it is the aim of this part of the study to characterize the psychological processing of a conditional relation, each experiment to be reported is a different approach towards this goal. This part consists of three chapters.

The first chapter concerns the meaning of the conditional conjunctions; the question is how conditional conjunctions are interpreted in natural language. Two experiments have been performed as two different approaches towards the description of the meaning of a conditional relation. The first experiment was a reasoning experiment. Subjects were presented with a conditional sentence as the first premise and one of the propositions as the second premise. They had to draw the conclusion. Based on the conclusion of the subject, one can infer the relational meaning of a conditional sentence. In the second experiment the meaning of a conditional sentence was approached in a rather direct way. Subjects had to judge conditional sentences with respect to the similarity of meaning. This experiment concerns the nature of the communication in a conditional sentence.

The second chapter of this study deals with the question of how a conditional relation is stored and transformed over time, and how it is reproduced. This question touches upon the problem of whether one conjunction is more basic than another. The approach selected in this chapter is a memory experiment.

The third chapter is concerned with conditional sentences from an information processing point of view. Time estimates are obtained for the factors that appeared important in the previous experiments, and a description is given of the processes of understanding conditional sentences.

Chapter 6   On the Interpretation of Conditional Conjunctions

One may distinguish conditional sentences depending on whether they express a material implication or an equivalence. Conditional sentences are frequently represented in logic as *if p then q* where p and q are propositions: p is a sufficient condition for q, while q is a necessary condition for p. In terms of a truth table: *p and q* is true, *p and not-q* is false, *not-p and q* is true and *not-p and not-q* is true. In terms of syllogistic reasoning this means that given *if p then q* from p follows q and from *not-q* follows *not-p*; from *not-p* no conclusion can be drawn with respect to q or *not-q* and from q no conclusion can be drawn with respect to p or *not-p*. This interpretation of a conditional relation is commonly called material implication. If a conditional relation is interpreted as equivalence, then *p and q* is true, *not-p and not-q* is true, *not-p and q* is false, *p and not-q* is false. Given *if p then q*, from p follows q and vice versa; from *not-p* follows *not-q* and vice versa. This relation is also called a biconditional relation. The terms conditional and biconditional in this study will denote material implication and equivalence, respectively.

"Correct" interpretation of conditional sentences by children. Several authors have investigated the development of the logical ability in children. In many of these studies the question was: At what age do children learn to reason according to the rules of logic? The material implication was considered as the correct interpretation of a conditional sentence. ROBERGE (1970) presented children of age 10 to 16 with complete syllogisms. They had to judge the validity of the conclusions. It appeared that children of all ages made the largest number of errors in judging syllogisms in which the correct answer was "indeterminate". No analysis is given of the kind of logically incorrect answers.

Also in studies of HILL (1961); O'BRIEN and SHAPIRO (1968); SHAPIRO and O'BRIEN (1970), and ROBERGE and PAULUS (1971) a response was considered correct of it conformed to the truth function of material implication. ROBERGE and PAULUS presented children of grade levels four, six, eight, and ten with class and conditional reasoning problems. There appeared to be a growth in reasoning over the grade levels. But no specification is given of the particular answers for the different logical forms. Thus, no conclusion emerges with respect to the interpretation of conditional sentences by these children. In SHAPIRO and O'BRIEN (1970) most errors were due to the biconditional interpretation of *if ... then*.

According to some authors (INHELDER and PIAGET, 1958; MATALON, 1962), adults are able to handle conditional sentences in a logical way, but children before the stage of formal operations are not able to do so. MATALON presented conditional sentences to children 10 years old. They were asked to draw conclusions, given a second premise, e.g., *if the red light is lit, the green light is lit; the red light is lit; what can be concluded with respect to the green light?*. They also had to indicate with respect to each combination of events (*p and q; p and not-q; not-p and q; not-p and not-q*) whether that combination can occur or not. The third task the children had to perform was to enumerate to themselves the possible and impossible combinations. The easiest task was to recognize the possible combinations (*p and q; not-p and q; not-p and not-q*) and to make the inference called "modus ponens" (*p therefore q*). A more difficult task was to recognize the impossible combination (*p and not-q* and the "modus tollens" (*not-q therefore not-p*). The most difficult task was to enumerate the possible and impossible combinations and to draw the correct conclusion in case the second premise was *not-p* or *q*. It appeared that most of the errors children made were due to the fact that *if* was interpreted as *if and only if*: the conditional conjunction was understood as if it was a biconditional conjunction in these cases. MATALON concludes that young children interpret conditional sentences as biconditional sentences. It is only at the age of 12 years or more that children will interpret the relation of implication in natural language in a logical way, according to MATALON.

PARIS (1975) has investigated the development of logical connectives. Children in grades two to eleven and adults were presented with pairs of pictures, each picture of a pair representing a scene. Sentences expressing a logical relation between the two scenes had to be judged as true or false with respect to the pair of pictures. An answer was considered to be an error if it did not conform to the laws of logic; the criterion for *if ... then* sentences was material implication. Almost all subjects of all ages (93%) judged a sentence as false if *p* was false and *q* true, in agreement with the biconditional interpretation of conditional sentences.

The studies discussed so far concerned children's logical thinking with conditionals. An answer was logically correct if it conformed to the truth table of material implication. Some of the studies did not even analyze the so-called errors which, however, are at least as interesting as the correct answers.

   Interpretation of conditional sentences by children. PEEL (1967) has studied how certain logical connectives are interpreted by children from 5 up to 10 years old. He did not postulate that material implication is the correct interpretation of a conditional relation. The experiment consisted of simple games between the experimenter and the child. The games differed with respect to the rule of the game. The rule was expressed in one of three ways: impli- cation (if ... then), incompatibility (if ... then not), and disjunction (either ... or). The results on the implication game indicated that *if ... then* is understood by children of all ages as *if and only if ... then*. On the other hand, when children in another task have to judge the acceptability of combinations, there appears to be a growth towards reasoning according to the truth table of material implication. The majority of children of age 5 judged the combination *not-p and q* as unacceptable, which is in agreement with the logical relation of equivalence; at the age of 11 years, however, the majority of the children judged this combination as acceptable, in accor- dance with the logical relation of material implication. These differences between the two tasks are similar to those found by MATALON: when children had to draw the correct conclusion, the behavior conformed to the relation of equivalence; when they had to judge the possibility of the different com- binations, their behavior conformed more the relation of material implication. Another result obtained by PEEL was that the concept of disjunction was in- terpreted by children 11 years old in the exclusive form (either ... or ... and not both) and not in the inclusive form (either ... or ... or both). It should be kept in mind that the exclusive *or* is equivalent to *if and only if* with a negation added to one of the propositions; the inclusive *or* is equiv- alent to *if* with an added negation, as will be discussed later.

   Another study that did not start on the a priori assumption that material implication is the correct interpretation of a conditional sentence was done by TAPLIN et al. (1974). Subjects from third grade to eleventh grade were required to evaluate the conclusion of several conditional arguments. Sub- jects of all age groups interpreted *if ... then* sentences most frequently as biconditional sentences. Some other interpretations occurred, however. From grade three until grade seven a decreasing number of subjects interpreted an *if ... then* sentence as the conjunction *and*; form grade seven until grade eleven an increasing number of subjects interpreted *if ... then* sentences as conditionals.

In studies by O'BRIEN et al. (1971) subjects had to evaluate the conclusion of a syllogistic reasoning task. It appeared that *if ... then* sentences are interpreted predominantly as biconditionals. With increasing age from grade four to grade ten this interpretation tends to be superseded, but only to a very small extent, by a conditional interpretation. Comparable results are reported in SHAPIRO and O'BRIEN (1970). This tendency was much more pronounced in other studies of these authors, cited in O'BRIEN et al. (1971).

Interpretation of conditional sentences by adults. Not only children but adults as well often do not interpret an *if ... then* sentence as an expression of a material implication. In a study by TAPLIN (1971) and by TAPLIN and STAUDENMAYER (1973) students had to evaluate the truth of conditional arguments. The majority of subjects who consistently assessed the validity of the arguments in a truth functional way interpreted a conditional sentence as an expression of a biconditional relation. However, when subjects were given three response alternatives - always true, sometimes true, never true - the majority of the subjects interpreted an *if ... then* sentence as a conditional. This was attributed by TAPLIN and STAUDENMAYER to the particularities of the task. The presence of the category "sometimes true" suggested to the subjects that this answer was appropriate in this task.

Conditionals have been extensively studied by WASON and JOHNSON-LAIRD (1972). They suggest that both material implication and equivalence are unsatisfactory interpretations of a conditional sentence. In one study (JOHNSON-LAIRD and TAGARD, 1969) evidence was found for a defective truth table. Subjects were presented with a conditional sentence, for convenience expressed here as *if p then q*, where *p* and *q* referred to properties of a card. Subjects were required to classify cards according to whether they indicated that the sentence was true or false, or whether they were irrelevant to the truth value of the sentence. The sentence was judged "true" with respect to cards with *p and q*, "false" with respect to cards with *p and not-q*, and irrelevant with respect to cards with *not-p and q* as well as cards with *not-p and not-q*. So, a conditional sentence is true if the antecedent and the consequent are true; the sentence is false if the antecedent is true and the consequent is false; the sentence does not have a truth value if the antecedent is false. LEGRENZI (1970) did a similar experiment, but used a binary situation, i.e., a situation where both the antecedent and the consequent could be falsified in only one way. Moreover, the situation possessed a temporal component. LEGRENZI found that subjects interpreted a conditional sentence as a biconditional sentence, contrary to the results of JOHNSON-LAIRD and TAGARD.

Interpretation of conditional conjunctions in different contexts. Conditional relations can be expressed not only with the conjunction *if then* but also with the conjunctions *unless, or, only if,* and others. From a logical point of view the following sentences are equivalent in the sense that they express the same relation between the same events:

if it is raining, the streets are wet;
if the streets are not wet, it is not raining;
it is not raining, unless the streets are wet;
either the streets are wet or it is not raining;
it is raining, only if the streets are wet.

It is, however, an open question as to whether these sentences are equivalent in natural language, too. The sentence *it is not raining, unless the streets are wet* may sound strange or may even be false for some people, because they claim that this sentence would imply that the streets are wet only if it is raining, and that sentence is not true. This would indicate that the conjunction *unless* is appropriately used only in a context where not only *if p then q* is true but also *if q then p*. Thus, it is suggested that a conditional relation is more readily interpreted as a biconditional relation when the relation is expressed with the conjunction *unless* than with the conjunction *if then*. One could ask whether the conjunctions *only if* and *or* are similar in this respect to *unless*.

The interpretation of a conditional conjunction depends also on the topic of the sentences. The sentence *if it is raining, the streets are wet* is less likely to be interpreted as a biconditional sentence, than the sentence *if it is freezing, the temperature is below $32^{\circ}F$.* According to NAESS (1962) the meaning of *or* depends on the topic of the sentence, just as the meaning of *if ... then*: *or* can express a conditional and a biconditional relation. One commonly uses the words inclusive and exclusive to indicate these interpretations of *or*. The sentence *p or q* in its exclusive interpretation is false on the occurrence of *p and q* as well as on the occurrence *not-p and not-q*. It is equivalent to the sentence *if and only if not-p then q*. The sentence *p or q* in its inclusive interpretation is false only on the occurrence of *not-p and not-q*. It is equivalent to the material implication in *if not-p then q*. LAKOFF (1971) discusses the same distinction in terms of symmetric and asymmetric *or*. An example of the symmetric *or* is the sentence *either John eats meat, or Harry eats fish*. This sentence is equivalent to the combination of both the following sentences: *if John does not eat meat, then Harry eats fish; if John eats meat, then Harry does not eat fish.* This *or* is exclusive: it is not possible that both *John eats meat* and *Harry eats fish* are true. The sentence *either Seymour eats his dinner, or his mother complains to the neighbors* is an example of the asymmetric *or*. This sentence is equivalent to *if Seymour does not eat his dinner, then his mother complains to the neighbors*. This *or* is inclusive: it is possible that Seymour eats his dinner and that his mother complains to the neighbors.

The meaning of *unless* is, according to REICHENBACH (1947), logically equivalent to *if not ... then; unless* can express a biconditional relation as well as a conditional relation.

Summarizing, the present study is concerned with thinking and natural language processing. The question is how people process conditional relations. Therefore, object of study is not whether people think logically; no a priori criterion is adopted for a good or false conclusion. In this respect it differs from some of the studies reported.

The main conclusion from the studies on child reasoning is that *if ... then* sentences are predominantly interpreted as biconditionals, although some studies indicated an increase over ages of the conditional interpretation. The question, then, is how adults interpret conditional sentences. The present study is not concerned with children but only with adults.

Because the primary concern of the present study is reasoning in natural language, some consequences for the selection of the material and of the tasks follow. First, the material consists of meaningful propositions instead of rather abstract symbols such as letters (TAPLIN and STAUDENMAYER, 1973). Second, in order to investigate the influence of contextual knowledge on the interpretation of conditionals, sentences from different contexts have been used. Third, several conditional conjunctions have been used. Finally, in order to study more directly deductive reasoning in natural language, a deductive reasoning task has been used and not, e.g., an evaluation task, where subjects have to evaluate the truth of a conditional sentence, or a selection task, where subjects have to choose instances in order to determine whether the sentence is true or false (WASON, 1968; WASON and JOHNSON-LAIRD, 1972; LEGRENZI, 1970; BRÉE and COPPENS, 1972; BRÉE and MEERUM-TERWOGT, 1971; VAN DUYNE, 1974).

6.1 Experiment I

This experiment, which has been reported earlier (NOORDMAN, 1972), concerns the question of how conditional conjunctions are interpreted in simple reasoning tasks in natural language. A deductive reasoning task has been used: subjects were presented with a conditional sentence as the first premise and one proposition as the second premise. They were required to draw the conclusion. Based on the conclusion made by the subject, one can infer how the relation has been interpreted.

The following conjunctions have been studied: *if ... then, either ... or, unless,* and *only if.* It is expected that these conjunctions are predominantly interpreted as biconditional conjunctions. Based on intuitive judgments on the acceptability of conditional sentences as has been described earlier, it is expected that there is a difference between these conjunctions: sentences with *unless, either ... or,* and *only if* will more readily be interpreted as biconditionals than sentences with *if ... then.*

Another aspect of the present study is the context of the sentences. The question is: To what extent does the interpretation of the conjunctions depend on the factual knowledge one has about the topic of the sentences and to what extent on the meaning of the conjunctions themselves? Because of the knowledge one has about the facts expressed in the two propositions, one knows that the relation between the facts in some cases is actually a biconditional relation, e.g., *it it is freezing, the temperature is below $32^\circ F$.* In other cases this relation is a conditional relation, e.g., *if it is raining, the streets are wet.* In still other cases the relation between the two facts is quite arbitrary; knowledge about the facts expressed in the two propositions of the sentence does not give any information about the question whether the relation is a conditional or a biconditional one, e.g., *if the red light is lit, the blue light is lit.* These types of sentences will be called sentences with a biconditional context, sentences with a conditional context, and sentences with an arbitrary context, respectively. In sentences with an arbitrary context the only information about the relation between the two events is the information conveyed by the conjunctions themselves. These sentences were included in order to single out the influence of the context from the influence of the conjunctions in the interpretation of the sentences. It was hypothesized that the conjunctions are generally interprete in a biconditional way in each of the three kinds of sentences, but that this would be the case in the sentences with a biconditional context more than in those with an arbitrary context and in the sentences with a conditional context less than in those with an arbitrary context.

Another question regards the ease with which one understands the conjunctions: do sentences expressed with different conjunctions differ in ease of understanding? Sentences with an arbitrary context were used in the experimen in order to investigate to what extent people make use of knowledge on the conjunctions independently of knowledge on the facts expressed in the propositions when they try to understand conditional sentences. If knowledge of the facts increases the ease of understanding conditional sentences, one would expect that sentences with an arbitrary context are more difficult to understand than the other types of sentences.

6.1.1 Method

Material. Twelve *if ... then* sentences have been constructed: four sentences had a biconditional context, four a conditional context, and four an arbitrary context. For each sentence three logically equivalent sentences have been constructed using the conjunctions *unless, either ... or,* and *only if*. Because *unless* is a negative conjunction, one of the propositions of an *if p then q* sentence has to be negated when that sentence is expressed with *unless*. In order to avoid a difference in the number of negative propositions between *if ... then* sentences and *unless* sentences, *p* was a negative proposition in about one-half of the *if p then q* sentences. The resulting 48 sentences, combinations of the twelve topics and four conjunctions, constituted the first premise for the experimental times. Each sentence was paired with one of the four possible propositions as second premise: *p, not-p, q, not-q* in the following way. For each of the three contexts a 4 x 4 Latin square was used with conjunctions, nature of second proposition, and sentence topic as the factors. The order of the presentation of the four conjunctions was balanced using twelve permutations of four elements. The number of items between any two items with the same topic was constant. The experimental items were preceded by two practice items.

It should be noted that the symbols *p, q, not-p,* and *not-q* were not presented in the experiment. They serve only as convenient representations of the propositions or clauses that constituted the material in the experiment.

Subjects. The subjects were 28 undergraduate students in psychology from the University of California at Berkeley. All these students were native-born speakers of the English language; they had no previous training in logic.

Procedure. The experiment was conducted during a class meeting. The two premises of each item together with the serial number of the item were presented with a slide projector. This presentation lasted 25 s. The subjects indicated their answer on a sheet of paper. This paper contained three answer alternatives for each item. The first alternative (a) was always the positive form of the proposition that was not used as second premise. The second answer alternative (b) was always the negation of (a). The third alternative (c) was always the word *indeterminate*. The order of the presentation of the answer alternatives was kept constant in order to reduce experimental error due to the difficulty of finding the answer alternatives. The three answer alternatives for an item were preceded by a serial number corresponding to the number of the item. The subjects were instructed to derive the correct conclusion from the two premises and to mark the letter of the corresponding alternative on their sheet.

6.1.2 Results

The first question to be treated is whether conditional sentences are interpreted as biconditional sentences (equivalence) or as conditional sentences (material implication). This question regards only those 24 items where the second premise is *not-p* or *q*. According to a conditional interpretation, the conclusion for those items is *indeterminate*; according to a biconditional interpretation, the conclusion is determinate: *not-q* if the second premise is *not-p* and *p* if the second premise is *q*. For each of the 24 items the number of determinate answers (*not-q* or *p*) is compared with the number of *indeterminate* answers by means of a chi-square test.

The eight items with a biconditional context were more frequently interpreted as biconditional sentences than as conditional sentences, the level of significance for each separate item being at least 0.005. The more interesting items are those in which the context is neutral with regard to the interpretation, or where it even suggests a conditional interpretation. Seven out of the eight items with an arbitrary context and six out of the eight items with a conditional context were more frequently interpreted as biconditionals than as conditionals, the level of significance being at least 0.05. Only two items were interpreted just as frequently in the conditional way as in the biconditional way. These were the two *if p then q, not-p* items; they will be discussed later.

Table 6.1 represents the degree of biconditionality of the different conjunctions. The data are obtained by subtracting the number of indeterminate answers from the number of determinate answers and summing these scores for each two items with the same context and conjunction. The maximum score of 56 would have been obtained if all subjects had interpreted the two items in a conjunction-context combination as biconditionals. The minimum score of -56 would have been obtained if all subjects had interpreted the two items as conditionals. The fact that all scores are positive indicates that the conjunctions are interpreted more frequently as biconditionals than as conditionals.

Table 6.1. Degree of biconditionality for items with different conjunctions in different contexts

Context	if...then	unless	Conjunction either...or	only if...then	mean
arbitrary	18	35	28	29	28
biconditional	32	43	36	43	39
conditional	18	34	29	35	29
mean	23	37	31	36	

Note: Maximum score = 56 (biconditional interpretation).
Minimum score = -56 (conditional interpretation).

The hypotheses on the difference in biconditionality between the conjunctions as well as between the contexts have been tested with parameter-free tests on the just-described biconditionality scores, computed per subject. In these tests, however, only the subjects are a random factor. In order to test the ability to generalize over language material as well, values of *min F'* have been computed (CLARK, 1973c). The data for this analysis of variance form a fractional design in which material is confounded with context. Therefore, both material and context are treated as random factors when testing the difference between conjunctions; both material and conjunctions are treated as random factors when testing the difference between contexts; the sentences are matched with respect to the positive versus negative character of the first premise. There is a difference in the interpretation of the four conjunctions. The conjunctions *unless, either ... or* and *only if* are almost to the same extent interpreted as biconditionals and more so than *if ... then*: Wilcoxon matched-pairs signed-ranks $z = 2.10$, $p < 0.02$ one tail; $min F'$ $(1,41) = 3.91$, $p < 0.05$ one tail. In sentences with a biconditional context, the conjunctions are interpreted more frequently as biconditionals than in sentences with an arbitrary context: Wilcoxon $z = 2.38$, $p < 0.01$ one tail; $min F'$ $(1,27) = 3.66$, $p < 0.05$ one tail. Surprisingly, the sentences with a conditional context are interpreted as biconditional sentences as frequently as the sentences with an arbitrary context.

Up to this point, attention has been paid to the interpretation of individual items. One may ask whether answers are perhaps consistently given according to an implicit truth table for conditional sentences. For a conjunction-context combination there are four different items: the second premise can be *p*, *q*, *not-p*, or *not-q*. For each of the 12 conjunction-context combinations the answers given by each subject to these four items have been tabulated as a sequence, ordering the items on the basis of the second premise: *p*, *q*, *not-p*, *not-q*. There are 28 subjects and consequently 28 x 12 = 336 such sequences of answers. Almost one-half - 156 - of these sequences are *q*, *p*, *not-q*, *not-p*, in conformance with the biconditional interpretation. Only 14 sequences conform to material implication (*q*, *indeterminate*, *indeterminate*, *not-p*). The pattern *q*,*p*, *indeterminate*, *indeterminate* - called positive equivalence - occurs only 15 times. There are only three other sequences that occur more than 10 times. They can best be described as deviations from the pattern of the biconditional interpretation in only one respect: in 24 cases the answer *indeterminate* replaces the answer *p*; in 21 cases the answer *indeterminate* replaces *not-q*; in 13 cases the answer *indeterminate* replaces *not-p*. Practically no subject gave evidence of a consistent interpretation of a conjunction in all three contexts other than the biconditional interpretatio

It has already been mentioned that *if ... then* is less biconditional than the other conjunctions. This difference is mainly due to the items *if p then q*, *not-p*. These items, when used in an arbitrary context and in a conditional context, are interpreted just as frequently in the coditional way as in the biconditional way. The data for the *if ... then* items and the *only if* items in both contexts are presented in Table 6.2. The answer for the items *if p then q*, *q* were more in agreement with a biconditional interpretation than the answers for the items *if p then q*, *not-p*: *p* was more frequently given as the answer in the first item than *not-q* in the second item. This difference, tested with the McNemar test, was significant both for the conditional contexts: $\chi^2(1) = 6.75$, $p < 0.01$, and for the arbitrary contexts: $\chi^2(1) = 12.07$, $p < 0.001$. This difference might be explained in the following way. The sentence *if p then q* relates the two propositions *p* and *q*. If one of the two propositions is presented as the second premise, the other is given as the answer. The situation is different if the second premise is *not-p*. That premise is not part of the sentence. There is no direct information available with respect to *not-p*. This is in agreement with results of WASON (1966) and JOHNSON-LAIRD and WASON (1970), who found that the proposition *not-p* is irrelevant to *q* or *not-q*. That the propositions *p* and *q* are more strongly related with each other than their negatives is also confirmed by the data on the two other items where the conditional and biconditional interpretation lead to the same results. The answer *q* for the item *if p then q*, *p* is given more frequently than the answer *not-p* for the item *if p then q*, *not-q*. This difference, tested with the McNemar test unless the binomial

Table 6.2. Frequency of answers in accordance with biconditional interpretation

Conjunction	Context	Second premise (first line) and conclusion (second line)			
		p q	q p	not-p not-q	not-q not-p
if ... then	arbitrary	28(0)	25(3)	11(15)	13(12)
	conditional	28(0)	23(4)	13(14)	21(7)
only if ... then	arbitrary	28(0)	22(5)	19(7)	28(0)
	conditional	28(0)	22(6)	23(4)	27(1)

Note: Maximun score = 28.

In parentheses the number of answers *indeterminate*.

test was required because of the small number of observations, was significant both for the conditional contexts ($p < 0.02$, binomial test) and for the
arbitrary contexts ($\chi^2(1) = 13.07$, $p < 0.001$). These results show that *if ...
then* sentences are to a certain extent interpreted as indicating a bidirectional relation between the two propositions stated in the sentence, but not
between the negations of these propositions. In other words *if ... then* sentences are sometimes interpreted not as an equivalence relation, but only as
a positive equivalence relation (see also BRÉE, 1973; BRÉE and MEERUM-TERWOGT,
1971). In this respect the conjunction *if ... then* differs from *only if*. The
difference found between the items *if p then q, q* and *if p then q, not-p* is
not found between the items *p only if q, q* and *p only if q, not-p*. In fact
the frequency of the answer *not-q* for the item *p only if q, not-p* is equal
to the frequency of the answer *p* for the item *p only if q, q*. Furthermore
not-q leads more frequently to the conclusion *not-p* and vice versa when the
first premise is *p only if q* than when the first premise is *if p then q*.
These differences were tested with the McNemar test unless the number of observations was so small as to require the binomial test: $\chi^2(1) = 13.07$, $p <
0.001$ and $\chi^2(1) = 4.90$, $p < 0.05$ for arbitrary contexts; $p = 0.07$ with the
binomial test and $\chi^2(1) = 5.78$, $p < 0.05$ for conditional contexts. These
data suggest that the meaning of the conjunction *only if* can be represented
both by a bidirectional relation between the two propositions stated in the

conditional sentences, as is the case for *if ... then*, and by a bidirectional relation between the negations of these propositions. This is in agreement with the analysis of *only*, given by HORN (1969). *Only John came* presupposes that John came and asserts that nobody else came. Consequently, the sentence *it is raining only if the streets are wet* asserts *if the streets are not wet, it is not raining*. The data indicate that this assertion is actually computed by the subject. The presence of this assertion in *only if* sentences constitutes the difference in biconditionality between *only if* sentences and *if ... then* sentences.

The results with respect to the conjunctions *if ... then* and *only if* can be interpreted in a way analogous to the given-new contract (CLARK, 1973b; HAVILAND and CLARK, 1974). If the sentence *if p then q* has been processed, both p and q as well as the bidirectional relation between them are stored information. In case the second premise is p, or q, this information is identical to a proposition in the first premise. That proposition is the antecedent and the integration is easily made. In case, however, the second premise is *not-p or not-q*, the listener[1] has to bridge the gap from this information to an appropriate antecedent. This requires the additional operation of adding a negation to the proposition in the first premise. And apparently some subjects fail this operation. The processes are different for *only if* sentences. In case an *only if* sentence has been processed, not only the propositions in the sentence but also their negations are stored information. The assertion in fact relates these negations.

Having discussed the question of how the conjunctions are interpreted, now the problem of the ease of understanding the conjunctions will be treated. The question is whether different contexts and different conjunctions differ as to the ease of understanding the conditional relation. These ease of understanding the conjunctions is inversely related to the number of errors. An answer is considered to be false in case both the biconditional and conditional interpretation of the conjunction do not allow that answer to be the conclusion. This definition is used for the sentences with a biconditional context as well as for the other sentences; a conditional interpretation of a conjunction in a biconditional context was not considered to be false. One qualification is made for the *if ... then* sentences: an answer for an *if ... then* item is considered correct if it conforms to the positive equivalence

---

[1] The terms *speaker* and *listener* are used to denote the producer and the receiver, respectively, of a message, and do not aim at a distinction between modalities of information transmission.

interpretation of the *if ... then* sentence. Examples of errors are the answer *indeterminate* or *not-q* when the second premise is p; the answer *not-p* when the second premise is q.

Using just these criteria for a correct interpretation of a conditional sentence, the number of errors on the four items in each conjunction-context combination was determined per subject. The number of errors, added up on the subjects, are presented in Table 6.3. There are almost no errors for the conjunctions *if ... then* and *only if*: less than 3%. The number of errors for the conjunctions *unless* and *either ... or* is 12 and 23%, respectively. The number of errors is greater in sentences with an arbitrary context than in other sentences: Wilcoxon matched-pairs signed-ranks $z = 3.65$, $p < 0.001$ for *unless* and $z = 3.64$, $p < 0.001$ for *either ... or*. This might be interpreted in the following way. The processing of the conjunctions *unless* and *either ... or* requires a large amount of computation. Added to the difficulty in processing the arbitrary material, which can hardly be comprehended, this results in an increase of the number of errors. An analogous explanation has been given by SHERMAN (1976) for the observation that the difficulty in comprehension of *sad* and *unhappy* depends on the complexity of the sentence.

Table 6.3. Number of errors for the items with different conjunctions and different contexts

| Context | Conjunction | | | | |
	if...then	unless	either...or	only if...then	mean
arbitrary	5	30	38	3	19
biconditional	2	3	18	5	7
conditional	2	6	22	2	5

Note: Maximum score = 112.

6.1.3 Discussion

The conjunctions tend to be interpreted as biconditional conjunctions, even if the context suggests a conditional interpretation. Knowledge of the facts in a sentence with a conditional context does not prevent subjects from interpreting the sentence in a biconditional way. One example is: *the car is running, only if there is gasoline in the tank*; more than 75% of the subjects concluded from *there is gasoline in the tank* that the car is running. Apparently the presence of gasoline is considered not as a necessary but as a sufficient condition for the running of the car. It might be argued that such a sentence is normally used in a situation where the speaker and the listener know that all the conditions for the running of the car have been fulfilled except perhaps one: the presence of gasoline. In other words it is suggested that such a sentence is uttered only in a context which is in fact a biconditional context. This suggestion is in agreement with the phenomenon of invited inference, discussed by GEIS and ZWICKY (1971). For the listener of the sentence *if you help me, I'll give you two dollars* it is clear that he will not get two dollars if he will not help the speaker. These results fit with the theory of GRICE (1967) on conversation. He discusses a conversation as a contract between the speaker and the listener. They cooperate in keeping the conversation going. One of the cooperative principles in this contract is the maxim of quantity: make your contribution to the conversation as informative as is required. The speaker has to convey all the relevant information; not doing so results in disturbing the conversation. Accordingly, the speaker of a conditional sentence is cooperative only if the necessary conditions he does not mention are irrelevant or satisfied. Otherwise he would in fact violate the maxim of quantity.

The upshot of this analysis is that the meaning of a conditional sentence is not determined exclusively by the sentence itself. All kinds of pragmatic factors play a role; there are conditions of application of a conditional sentence, i.e., the situation has to be such that the speaker and the listener know that there is a biconditional relation between the antecedent and the consequent.

Consequently, it should be noted in passing that people do not violate the rules of logic when they interpret a conditional sentence not as material implication but as equivalence. If the relation between the antecedent and the consequent in the conversational context is in fact, due to all kinds of pragmatic factors, a biconditional relation, then people think logically when they interpret a conditional sentence as a biconditional sentence. Any account of the thinking process that does not deal with the pragmatics of the conversation will be insufficient or even misleading.

6.2 Experiment II

A conditional sentence expresses the relation between two states or events. This relation can be characterized by specifying the inferences one can make from one state or event with respect to the other one. This constitutes part of the meaning of a conditional sentence. This inferential aspect has been studied in Experiment I. In the present experiment the meaning of conditional sentences has been studied in a somewhat different way. In this experiment the conditional relation between two events has been expressed by means of several conjunctions. Sentences were presented pairwise. Subjects had to judge whether the sentences in a pair had the same or a different meaning.

6.2.1 Method

Material. Two sets of sentences have been used. The sentences are presented in Table 6.4. The sentences in the first set express the conditional relation between paying the examination fee and obtaining a driver's licence. The sentences in the second set express the conditional relation between the temperature and the freezing of water. The first set of sentences expresses a conditional relation, the second set expresses a biconditional relation. Each set consists of six sentences. One sentence is constructed with the conjunc-

Table 6.4. Sets of sentences used in Experiment II

Set 1

1. if John got his driver's licence,	he paid the examination fee
2. if John did not pay the examination fee,	he did not get his driver's licence
3. John did not get his driver's licence,	unless he paid the examination fee
4. either John paid the examination fee,	or he did not get his driver's licence
5. John got his driver's licence,	only if he paid the examination fee
6. John did not get his driver's licence,	if he did not pay the examination fee

Set 2

1. if the water was freezing,	the temperature was below $32^{O}F$
2. if the temperature was not below $32^{O}F$,	the water was not freezing
3. the water was not freezing,	unless the temperature was below $32^{O}F$
4. either the water was not freezing,	or the temperature was below $32^{O}F$
5. the water was freezing,	only if the temperature was below $32^{O}F$
6. the water was not freezing,	if the temperature was not below $32^{O}F$

---

tion *unless*, one with the conjunction *either* ... *or*, and one with the conjunction *only if*. Several sentences can be constructed with a particular conjunction; in all cases that sentence has been selected that seemed intuitively the most acceptable one. This selection has been made on the basis of acceptability judgments made by native speakers. Thus, the sentence *John did not get his driver's licence, unless he paid the examination fee* has been selected and not the sentence *John paid the examination fee, unless he did not get his driver's licence*. Because of special interest in the conjunction *if ... then*, three *if ... then* sentences have been added: one sentence containing two positive clauses, another sentence containing two negative clauses in reversed order, the third one containing two negative clauses with the place of the conjunction in the middle of the sentence.

Subjects. The same subjects as in Experiment I served as subjects in the present experiment. Both experiments were in fact conducted during the same class meeting; Experiment II was administered after Experiment I.

Procedure. The 15 pairs of sentences that can be constructed for each set were presented to the subjects on a sheet of paper. The pairs were presented in a random order. The subjects had to judge the similarity of meaning of the two sentences. If according to their intuitive feeling the two sentences expressed the same content, they had to mark "same", otherwise they had to mark "different".

6.2.2 Results and Discussion

For each set of sentences a matrix of dissimilarities has been constructed. These matrices have been analyzed with the nonmetric multidimensional scaling program Minissa-1 (N) of Roskam and Lingoes. A one-dimensional representation accounts for the data in both cases, as is shown in Table 6.5, panel a.

There are striking differences between the two sets of sentences. With respect to the first set of sentences, the only difference is between sentence 1 and the other sentences. This can be interpreted as a difference in the nature of the message of the conditional sentence. To illustrate, sentence 1 will be contrasted with sentence 2. Sentence 2 *if John did not pay the examination fee, he did not get his driver's licence*, expresses that not paying the fee is a condition or eventually a cause for not getting the licence. Sentence 1 however, *if John got his driver's licence, he paid the examination fee* does not express that getting the licence is a condition or cause for paying the fee. The message communicated in this sentence is that the listener may infer that John has paid the fee from the knowledge that he got his licence. The crucial difference is the order of the clauses with respect to the con-

Table 6.5. Two- and one-dimensional scaling solution for the two sets of sentences

Sen-tence	Panel a One-dimensional solution		Panel b Two-dimensional solution			
	set 1	set 2	set 1		set 2	
			I	II	I	II
1	2.24	-0.45	2.21	0.00	-0,46	-1.01
2	-0.45	-0.45	-0.45	-0.06	-0.56	0.62
3	-0.45	-0.45	-0.41	0.12	-0.16	-0.32
4	-0.45	2.24	-0.35	-0.20	1.71	-0.12
5	-0.45	-0.45	-0.38	0.16	0.11	0.77
6	-0.45	-0.45	-0.62	-0.02	-0.63	0.06

Note: stress ≤ 1.5%.

junction. An even clearer example is sentences in the present tense that dif-fer only with respect to this order: the sentence *if John is ill, he is not going to his work* expresses that John's being ill is a condition or eventu-ally a cause for not going to his work. The sentence *if John is not going to his work, he is ill* expresses that one may infer John's illness from John's not going to his work. In terms of condition and consequence: John's not going to his work is the condition for the listener's inference that John is ill. As far as the state of affairs expressed in the first sentence of both sentence pairs is concerned, one may say that what is cognitively the consequence is expressed in the *then* clause. In the second sentence of each pair, however, what is cognitively the consequence is expressed in the first clause, right after the conjunction *if*. From the consequence one infers to the condition. The first type of sentences may be said to express a condition-consequence relation and the second type of sentences an inference relation. It seems that the characterization of condition-consequence sentences and inference senten-ces, described in terms of the position in the sentence of that information that is cognitively the condition, is true more generally. The sentence *John is going to his work, unless he is ill* seems to express a condition-consequence relation and the sentence *John is ill, unless he is going to his work* an inference relation.

The difference between condition-consequence relations and inference relations may be formalized in the following way. If the condition or, for that matter, the cause is mentioned after the conjunction, the sentence expresses a condition-consequence relation. If the condition is mentioned in the other clause, the sentence expresses an inference relation. It should be noted that the crucial point in this distinction is the place of the condition with respect to the place of the conjunction, irrespective of whether the conjunction is mentioned in the first or in the second clause. The observations with respect to the communicative nature of the sentences may be summarized as follows: The sentences differ with respect to the information which is supposed to be known and which information is intended to be inferred as new information. In a condition-consequence relation, the condition is the "topic" of the communication or the presupposed information; the consequence is the "comment" or the new information. In inference relations on the other hand, what is cognitively the consequence is the "topic" in the communication; the condition is the "comment" in the communication. For similar observations see SEUREN (1975, p.315 ff.).

The distinction between condition-consequence relations and inference relations may also be related to the function of the clauses as such. The function of the clause following the conditional conjunction is to express a condition and the function of the other clause to express a consequence. In an inference relation, however, the clause following the conjunction expresses what from a cognitive point of view is a consequence; the other clause expresses what from a cognitive point of view is a condition. There is, then, an incongruence between what is the condition and consequence according to the sentence and what is the condition and consequence from a cognitive point of view. This incongruence is solved, of course, when one realizes that the clause following the conditional conjunction expresses a condition for an inference.

In the first set of sentences, only sentence 1 expresses an inference relation. In this way it contrasts with the other sentences; these express a condition-consequence relation, although this is somewhat unclear for sentence 4

The results with respect to the second set of sentences are different (Table 6.5, panel a). The main contrast is clearly between sentence 4 and the other five sentences. From a cognitive point of view it is much less obvious than in the first set what the condition is and what the consequence is. One might argue that the temperature being below 32^{0}F is the condition for the freezing of the water. In that case, the sentence *if the water was freezing, the temperature was below 32°F* is an inference relation. These sentences do, however, more properly express an equivalence by definition, between freezing and the temperature of the water. Accordingly, the difference found for the first set of sentences should have diminished or disappeared. The difference that is found can best be interpreted as a difference in surface structure: sentence 4 is the only sentence with the coordinate conjunction. This syntactic difference was overruled by the semantic difference in the first set of sentences.

The two-dimensional solution (Table 6.5, panel b) for set 1 sentences leads to the same interpretation as the one-dimensional solution. The two-dimensional solution for set 2 sentences yields some additional information. The second dimension weakly reflects the contrast between condition-consequence relations and an inference relation.

The present experiment highlights an aspect of the meaning of conditional sentences that could not show up in the first experiment. Subjects are sensitive to the semantic difference between inference relations and condition-consequence relations. This may be seen as a difference in the communicative nature of a conditional sentence, particularly a difference in the expected availability of information. In a condition-consequence sentence one infers from the condition to the consequence; knowledge about the condition is supposed by the speaker to be more readily available. In an inference sentence one infers from the consequence to the condition; knowledge about the consequence is supposed by the speaker to be more readily available.

Chapter 7   Storing Conditional Relations

Having discussed the way in which conditional conjunctions are interpreted, the next problem to be treated is how a conditional relation is stored and transformed over time, and how it is reproduced. Here the question arises as to whether one conditional conjunction is more basic than another in the sense that one is more likely to retain and reproduce a conditional relation in one conjunction rather than in another.

These questions will be studied by means of a memory experiment. Because in this experiment one is mainly interested in meaning preserving reproductions, one has to determine whether the reproduced material has the same meaning as the presented material. From the first experiment it is clear that a conditional sentence will often be interpreted in a biconditional way. Accordingly, when a conditional sentence is reproduced in a form that is equivalent to a biconditional interpretation of that sentence, the reproduced sentence is not to be considered as differing in meaning from the presented sentence. If the sentence *if it is raining, the streets are wet* is reproduced as *if the streets are wet, it is raining,* that reproduction is considered as a meaning preserving reproduction. In fact, it is assumed that the original sentence is interpreted on the assumption: other sources of the streets being wet are not under consideration. This amounts to the following rule: a reproduced sentence is considered to differ in meaning from the presented sentence if and only if the reproduced sentence is no paraphrase of the presented sentence, neither according to a biconditional interpretation nor according to a conditional interpretation of the presented sentence.

7.1 Experiment III

7.1.1 Method

Material. In this experiment no special attention is paid to the distinction between sentences with a conditional context and sentences with a biconditional context. The reason is not only that, according to the results of Experiment I, both conditional and biconditional sentences are predominantly interpreted as biconditional sentences, but mainly that the crucial distinction in a memory experiment is between meaningful and meaningless material. Sentences with an arbitrary context are considered to be meaningless in contrast to sentences with a contitional or biconditional context. These two kinds of sentences have been used in the present experiment. In the first kind of sentence the meaning of the two clauses does not convey any information about the conditional relation as such, whereas in the second kind of sentence the meaning of the two clauses conveys information about the conditional relation as such. The second variable of the material was the conjunction. Three conjunctions have been used: *if ... then...*, *... unless ...*, and *only if ... then ...*, the dots indicating the position of the clauses. The third variable of the material was the negativity of the clauses; both the first and the second clauses could be a negative, yielding four different kinds of sentences. With these three variables 24 different kinds of sentences are characterized. These 24 sentences constituted the material in the present experiment.

The 12 meaningful sentences have been presented to all subjects. With the 12 different types of meaningless sentences, 144 sentences have been constructed by pairing the 12 different types with 12 different topics. For each subject each sentence type was paired with another topic. Each of the 12 sets of sentences was presented to two subjects.

Procedure. The 24 sentences have been presented in three blocks of eight sentences each. Each block was balanced with respect to the three variables: meaningful vs meaningless sentences, conjunction, and negativity. The order of presentation of the sentences in each block was randomized; the order of presentation of the blocks was balanced over the subjects. The sentences were typed on 20 x 10 cm cards. Each sentence was presented for 20 s. The subject was instructed to study that sentence carefully and learn it by heart. After this learning phase the subject was required to count backwards by steps of 7 starting with a number between 800 and 1000. After about 1 min the subject was given 20 x 10 cm cards with two probes on each card, the one typed above the other. The two probes were two words, one out of each clause of a conditional sentence that was just learned. Those words have been selected that expressed most adequately the topic of the clause. The probes were mostly nouns. The subject was required to write down the sentence as accurately as possible. The subject was told that the upper probe could equally well be a word from the first clause as a word from the second clause. In fact, in one-half of the cases the order (above-below) of presentation of the probes was

90

parallel to the order (left-right) of the clauses. The order of probing the sentences was randomized for each subject. Between the reproduction phase of one block and the learning phase of the following block there was an interval of 3 min, during which the subject was given some comics to enjoy.

Subjects. The subjects were 24 university students from different disciplines. They were paid for their participation in the experiment.

7.1.2 Results

The number of meaning preserving, meaning changing, and deficient reproductions for both meaningful and meaningless material are represented in Table 7.1. A reproduction is considered to be deficient if it is not a conditional

Table 7.1. Reproduction of meaningful and meaningless conditional sentences

	Meaningful	Meaningless
meaning preserving reproductions[a]	266	205
- under biconditional interpretation	*266*	*205*
- under conditional and biconditional interpretation	*222*	*153*
- identical	*189*	*125*
meaning changing reproductions	9	66
no reproductions	13	17
total	288	288

[a] The inclusion relations between the three types of meaning preserving reproductions are described in the text.

sentence, i.e., if there is no conjunction, or if the reproduction contains only one clause or less. The meaning preserving reproductions can be subdivided into three classes. The first one contains the reproductions that are identical to the original sentences; the second class contains the reproductions that are paraphrases of the original sentences if these are interpreted as conditional sentences; the third class contains the reproductions that are paraphrases of the original sentences if these are interpreted as biconditional sentences. It is clear that the first class is included in the second one, and the second class in the third one. Based on the results of the first experiment, meaning preserving sentences are defined as those sentences that fall in class three, as has already been stated. Because the present experiment is concerned with the question of how the meaning of conditional sentences is stored, only those reproductions are studied in the following analyses that preserve the meaning of the original sentences.

The results have been analyzed by means of parameter-free tests. However, in order to have an idea about the generalizability of the results over both subjects and language material, values of $min\ F'$ are computed as well. This would hardly have been required for the meaningless sentences. The conventional statistics indicate rather well the ability to generalize to subjects and material, because the subjects were presented with different materials. In computing the $min\ F'$ values, not only the material but also the clause negativity had to be treated as a random factor, because of the confounding of these factors; the sentences were matched with respect to clause negativity.

Meaningful sentences are better retained than meaningless sentences. The number of meaning preserving reproductions was greater for meaningful sentences than for meaningless sentences: Wilcoxon matched-pairs signed-ranks $z = 4.11$, $p < 0.001$; $min\ F'\ (1,25) = 23.98$, $p < 0.001$.

The central question in this experiment is how the conjunctions are retained and reproduced. Table 7.2 indicates in terms of which conjunction the *if ... then, unless,* and *only if* sentences are reproduced. There is a clear tendency to reproduce the conditional sentences as *if ... then* sentences. Two phenomena account for this result. First, the conjunctions differ in their retention, as indicated by the diagonal cells; $\chi_r^2(2) = 14.18$, $p < 0.001$ for meaningful material and $\chi_r^2(2) = 8.13$, $p < 0.02$ for meaningless material, tested with the Friedman rank analysis; $min\ F'\ (2,27) = 5.06$, $p < 0.05$ for meaningful sentences and $min\ F'\ (2,29) = 3.25$, $p < 0.10$ for meaningless sentences. The conjunction *if ... then* is better retained than the conjunctions *unless* and *only if* both for meaningful (Wilcoxon matched-pairs signed-ranks $z = 2.00$, $p < 0.05$; $z = 3.53$, $p < 0.001$ and $min\ F'\ (1,27) = 5.89$, $p < 0.05$) and meaningless sentences (Wilcoxon $z = 2.64$, $p < 0.01$; $z = 2.98$, $p < 0.01$ and $min\ F'\ (1,29) = 6.23$, $p < 0.05$). Second, there are more transformations towards than from the conjunction *if ... then*. Sentences with the conjunction *unless* are more frequently reproduced as *if ... then* sentences than the other way around: Wilcoxon matched-pairs signed-ranks $z = 2.37$, $p < 0.02$ for meaning-

Table 7.2. Reproduction of meaningful and meaningless conditional sentences in terms of conditional conjunctions used

	Presented					
	Meaningful			Meaningless		
Reproduced	ifthen	unless	only ifthen	ifthen	unless	only ifthen
ifthen	84	10	32	63	14	23
unless	0	71	12	4	44	9
only ifthen	8	3	46	6	3	39

ful sentences and $z = 2.00$, $p < 0.05$ for meaningless sentences; $min\ F'$ (1,22) = 7.64, $p < 0.05$ for both kinds of sentences. Similarly, sentences with *only if* are more frequently reproduced as *if ... then* sentences than the other way around: Wilcoxon matched-pairs signed-ranks $z = 2.73$, $p < 0.01$ for meaningful material and $z = 2.31$, $p < 0.03$ for meaningless material; $min\ F'$ (1,24) = 12.26, $p < 0.01$ for both kinds of sentences.

Another interesting result concerns the order in which the two clauses of the original sentence are reproduced. It should be noted that changing the order of the clauses, just as well as , e.g., changing the place of a negative or adding or deleting two negatives, is a transformation that preserves the meaning of the presented sentence, if this sentence is interpreted as a biconditional sentence: both *if b then not a* and *if a then not b* are considered meaning preserving transformations of *if not a then b*.

The order of the clauses is very well preserved. In only 25 of the 266 reproductions of meaningful sentences has the order of the clauses been changed; for the meaningless sentences the order of the clauses is changed in only 30 of the 205 reproductions. The reversal of the clauses did not depend on whether the probes were presented in the same order in which they occurred in the sentence or in the opposite order: Wilcoxon matched-pairs signed-ranks $z = 1.13$, $p > 0.25$.

7.1.3 Discussion

Of the conjunctions studied in the present experiment, the conjunction *if ... then* is the most fundamental one, in the sense that people are inclined to express a conditional relation by means of that conjunction. One could argue that the results can be accounted for by the higher frequency of occurrence of *if ... then* in natural language: the more frequently a conjunction is used, the more it is available. This, however, is no explanation; higher frequency itself has to be explained. Actually, one could argue just as well that *if ... then* is more frequently used because it is cognitively less complex. In the following experiment an attempt will be made to specify the differences between the conjunctions in terms of the complexity of cognitive processes.

The systematic way in which the order of the clauses is reproduced deserves some closer examination. As has been discussed earlier, the order of the clauses contains some information about the nature of the relation. Inverting the order of the clauses with respect to the conjunction does not change the meaning as far as a biconditional truth table is concerned, but it changes the nature of the message conveyed by the conditional sentence from a condition-consequence relation into an inference relation or vice versa. This reversal of a condition-consequence relation into an inference relation or vice versa actually constitutes a reversal of the topic and the comment in the communication, as has been discussed above.

The results of the reversal of the order of the clauses can best be interpreted in the light of this distinction. Given the characterization of sentences as expressing a condition-consequence relation or an inference relation, one can ask how well these characteristics are understood and retained as such. All the meaningful sentences in the present experiment expressed a condition-consequence relation. For the meaningless sentences one cannot properly make this distinction because there are no grounds from a cognitive or conceptual point of view for deciding whether one clause expresses the condition and the other the consequence of a conditional relation. At best one can in some cases infer from a subject's reproduction whether he interpreted one clause as expressing the condition.

None of the 266 reproductions of the meaningful sentences changed the meaning from a condition-consequence to an inference relation. Thus, the information which cognitively is the condition is retained and reproduced as such. One can ask, however, whether the subject has merely retained the order of mentioning the clauses without retaining the condition and the consequence as such. If the sentence *if p then q* is reproduced as *if p then q* or as *only if p then q*, what is the condition in the original sentence is reproduced again as the condition. But this can be attributed merely to the fact that the subject has learned the sentence by heart and that he has retained the order of mentioning the clauses without realizing what is the condition and what the consequence. He has not necessarily retained the information that is the condition as the condition and the information that is the consequence as the consequence. Therefore, a stronger case is to consider only those reproductions that were transformations from *if ... then* or *only if* to *unless* or vice versa, in which the conjunction was replaced from one clause to the other, e.g., *John is going to his work, unless he is ill* to *if John is ill, he is not going to his work*. In these transformations a condition-consequence relation is retained as such only if the replacing of the conjunction is accompanied by the reversal of the clauses, so that the order of the clauses with respect to the conjunctions is not changed. There were 25 transformations from *if ... then* or *only if* to *unless* or vice versa. In all these transformations the order of the clauses was reversed and the position of the conjunction was changed. These 25 reversals were all the reversals that occurred in the experiment, as has been mentioned above. Thus, the information that is the condition is retained as such and the information that is the consequence is retained as such. Although the number of reversals is greater when the order (above-below) of the probes parallels their order (left-right) in the sentence (18) than when they are not parallel (7) - Wilcoxon matched-pairs signed-ranks $p < 0.05$ - the result that in both cases all the reproductions were reversals was significant: Wilcoxon matched-pairs signed-ranks $p < 0.001$ for the nonparallel probes and $p < 0.02$ for the parallel probes. It should be remembered that in general the order of the probes had no effect on the reversal of the clauses, as has been stated above. Consequently, the reversal of the clauses is not or at least not only due to the reversal of the probes, but also to the fact that the condition and the consequence are retained as such.

In the case of the meaningless sentences, there is no way for distinguishing condition-consequence relations from inference relations; one cannot speak of the retention of the condition and the consequence as such. It follows that the reversal of the order of the clauses, as observed for meaningful sentences, should not occur in the reproduction of the meaningless sentences. However, one may argue that the subject, when presented with the sentence, attributes to one clause the meaning of condition. The clause immediately following the conjunction might be the most likely one to be attributed the function of condition. In this conception of understanding a sentence, the interpretation of the conjunction has a key role: it directs a process of identifying the condition. In this case one expects that the reversal of the order of the clauses does occur in the above-mentioned cases. There were 30 reproductions that were transformations from *unless* to *if ... then* or *only if* or vice versa in which the conjunction was replaced from one clause to the other. In 18 cases also the order of the clauses has been reversed. In 12 cases the order of the clauses has remained unchanged. This difference is not significant: Wilcoxon matched-pairs signed-ranks, $z = 1.33$, $p > 0.10$. Consequently, it is not at the moment of understanding the sentence that one clause is attributed the meaning of the condition. This confirms the interpretation given for the meaningful sentences: the condition is understood as such and, therefore, reproduced as such.

A final remark should be made. One might argue that the reproduced meaningful sentences are condition-consequence relations, because only condition-consequence sentences have been used, and that at the moment of reproduction the retained material is expressed in a condition-consequence relation. This, of course, does not invalidate the conclusion that subjects understand and reproduce the information of the condition-consequence relation as such, as distinct from the information of an inference relation. In fact, the argument rests on this assumption.

The result with respect to the reversal of the order of the clauses supports the conclusion of the previous experiment. The distinction between inference relations and condition-consequence relations, which can be explained in terms of topic and comment, characterizes the meaning of conditional sentences and also the memory processes with these sentences.

Chapter 8   The Processing of Conditional Sentences

8.1 Experiment IV

The aim of the present experiment is to construct a model for the processing
of conditional sentences. The previous experiments revealed important factors
in processing conditional sentences. The question is: How completely do these
factors account for the mental processes when people understand conditional
sentences?

In the present experiment subjects were required to verify conditional sentences against their knowledge of the world. The RT was measured for the subject's judgment. Sentences have been constructed with the conjunctions *if ...
then* and *unless*; with positive and negative first and second clause. Both inference and condition-consequence sentences have been used.

In the present experiment one is mainly interested, of course, in the RTs
for the correct judgments. In deciding whether a judgment is correct or not,
one must know whether a conditional sentence is true or false. The criterion
for the truth of a conditional sentence has been derived from Experiment I.
On the basis of the results of Experiment I it is assumed that all sentences
are interpreted as biconditional sentences. The truth of a sentence is determined with respect to the biconditional interpretation. If, for example, a
sentence is true according to a conditional interpretation, but false according to a biconditional interpretation, that sentence is considered to be fals
For example, the sentence *if the stove is not burning, it is warm inside* is
considered to be false. There could be other causes for a warm temperature
than the (present) burning of the stove; therefore that sentence might be con
sidered true. Based on the results of Experiment I, however, it is assumed
that these other causes are not taken into consideration by the subject. More
over, the instruction made the biconditional interpretation even more obvious
In fact, the subjects have been instructed to judge whether the sentences are
generally true or false and not to search for special situations that might
verify or falsify the sentences.

Based in the results of Experiment III it is expected that sentences are easier to understand when expressed with the conjunction *if ... then* than with *unless*. A second hypothesis is derived from Experiment II and III and concerns the distinction between inference relations and condition-consequence relations. It is assumed that inference relations are more difficult to understand than condition-consequence relations. One might argue that an inference relation, *if q then p*, contains the embedding proposition *from* (q) *it can be inferred that* (p) *because if p then q*, which a condition-consequence relation does not contain. An inference relation expresses an inference as well as a condition-consequence relation as its background. This argument can be stated in another way. In the sentence *if p then q*, p is the condition and q the consequence. In a sentence that expresses an inference relation, the clause following the conditional conjunction expresses what cognitively is the consequence and the other clause expresses the condition. Consequently, there is an incongruence between what is the condition and the consequence according to the structure of the sentence and what is the condition and the consequence according to the knowledge of the listener and speaker. Handling this incongruence requires extra processing time. This incongruence can be solved in fact by processing the embedding proposition: *it can be inferred that* ... .

A third hypothesis is that sentences with a negative clause are more difficult than sentences with a positive clause. There should be a monotonic increase in RT from sentences with no negative clause, to sentences with one negative clause and to sentences both clauses of which are negative.

Finally, it is assumed that the RT for true sentences is shorter than for false sentences. From studies of NOORDMAN-VONK (1979; NOORDMAN-VONK and NOORDMAN, 1974) it is clear that people in verifying a statement search for confirming evidence earlier than for disconfirming evidence. She proposes a model for semantic judgments that accounts for the results in a variety of tasks. The essential property of that model is that a verfication process precedes a falsification process.

8.1.1 Method

Material. Sixteen different item types have been constructed by means of the following four dichotomic variables: the positive vs negative character of the first clause, similarly for the second clause, the fact whether the conjunction *if ... then* is used or *unless*, the fact whether the clauses are mentioned in one order or in the other. It should be remembered that changing the order of mentioning the clauses with respect to the conjunction changes a condition-consequence relation into an inference relation or vice versa. There were eight topics of sentences, i.e., the state of affairs dealt with by the conditional sentences. These eight topics consisted of two subgroups of four topics each. The topics of the first group were such that the sentence *if p then q* was true, e.g., *if the stove is burning, it is warm inside*. The topics of the second group were such that the sentence *if p then q* was false, e.g., *if John is ill he is going to his work*. The 16 sentence forms and the eight topics yield 128 sentences. It seemed advisable not to present a subject the same topic 16 times. Therefore, the items were divided into two groups of 64 items. Each subject was presented with only one group of items; this resulted in two groups of subjects. The following items were presented to the first group of subjects. The first four topics were realized as condition-consequence relations with *if ... then* and as inference relations with *unless*. The other four topics were realized as inference relations with *if ... then* and as condition-consequence relations with *unless*. The items for the other group of subjects were constructed the other way around. The items were administered in four blocks of 16 items each. The assignment of item topic to clause negativity (both clauses, only the first clause, only the second clause, none of the clauses) and to experimental block was achieved by means of four 4 x 4 Latin squares, one for each combination of conjunction and nature of the relation (condition-consequence vs inference). As a result of this procedure the items constituted a complete factorial design with conjunction, clause negativity, and nature of the relation as the factors. The topic and, consequently, the truth of the sentences was balanced with respect to these factors. The difference between the two groups of subjects was constituted by the fact that the combination of clause negativity, conjunction, and nature of the relation was true for one group of subjects and false for the other group, due to the difference in topic. Finally, the experimental blocks were balanced with respect to all factors. The experimental blocks were preceded by one practice block that was comparable in all respects to the experimental blocks. Only the topics of these sentences were different from those in the experimental blocks. The first item in each experimental block was a practice item, resulting in 17 items per block.

Subjects. The subjects were 20 students of different disciplines. The subjects volunteered in the experiment; they were paid for their participation.

Procedure. The items were presented with two projectors: the sentences were presented in one projector; the other projector projected a blank field during the time interval between the items. The sentences were clearly visible as black letters on a white field. They were presented as two rows, each clause constituting a row. The sentences subtended a visual angle of approximately 13 deg on the average. The equipment was the same as described in Part I.

The subject was required to judge whether, in general, the sentence was true or false; he was instructed not to search for special or sophisticated situations that might verify or falsify the sentence. He had to give the answer as quickly as possible without making errors. The answer was given by pressing one of two response buttons. For one-half of both groups of subjects the true button had to be pressed with the dominant hand, the false button with the other hand. For the other half of both groups of subjects, it was just the reverse. The subjects were required to keep their index fingers on the buttons. The time was measured from the onset of the presentation until the subject pressed a button. There was a 4 s interval between two items. Between two blocks of items there was an interval of approximately 1 min. At the end and at the beginning of each block the subject was given an auditory warning signal. The experiment lasted about 25 min.

8.1.2 Results

The percentage of errors averaged 11%. Subjects with more than 21% errors were not included in the analysis of the data. This resulted in the elimination of six subjects, leaving 20 subjects in the analysis.

There was a positive correlation between lenght of RT and number of errors: $r = 0.65$; $t(30) = 4.68$, $p < 0.001$. Both the number of errors and the length of the RT indicate the difficulty of an item.

Because of the large number of errors, the question arises as to whether there is a systematic pattern in the errors. One might ask, for example, whether some items are less likely interpreted as biconditionals than other items. Such a result, then, might be an indication for an interpretation other than the biconditional, e.g., the interpretation in conformance with material implication or positive equivalence. No such evidence was found, however. The only systematic result was that the highest number of errors was made in the *unless not* items. This might be explained by the double negation in these items. Some remarks with respect to these items will be made later.

For each of the 20 subjects 16 medians for the correct responses have been computed, one median for each item type. These medians have been analyzed in a six-way analysis of variance with repeated measures on four factors. These within subject factors are: conjunction, nature of the conditional relation and clause negativity for the first and for the second clause. The two between subject factors are constituted by the above described assignments of topics to item types and by the assignment of the yes response button to the dominant or nondominant hand. Because this latter factor had no effect on the RTs, it was dropped from the model.

Table 8.1. Mean RTs [ms] for the verification of conditional sentences

Conjunction					a
	Relation	++	-+	+-	--
if...then	condition-consequence	2480	3161	2883	3705
	inference	2750	3046	3253	3879
unless	condition-consequence	3213	3883	4227	4826
	inference	3792	4010	4380	5556

[a] + and - indicate positive and negative clause, respectively; order of signs corresponds to order of clause.

The means of the medians are presented in Table 8.1. The RT for *unless* sentences is 1091 ms longer than for *if ... then* sentences: $F_1(1,18)$ = 98.78, $p < 0.001$; *min* F' (1,16) = 43.72, $p < 0.001$. The RT for inference relations is 286 ms longer than for condition-consequence relations: $F_1(1,18)$ = 15.28, $p < 0.01$; *min* $F'(1,23)$ = 10.19, $p < 0.01$. The RT varies with clause negativit The RT is 636 ms longer when the first clause is a negative than when it is a positive: $F_1(1,18)$ = 45.16, $p < 0.001$; *min* $F'(1,19)$ = 23.48, $p < 0.001$. The similar effect for the second clause was 797 ms: $F_1(1,18)$ = 68.31, $p < 0.001$; *min* $F'(1,21)$ = 39.53, $p < 0.001$. There was only one additional effect: the interaction of the conjunctions with the positive vs negative character of the second clause: $F_1(1,18)$ = 8.03, $p < 0.05$; *min* $F'(1,21)$ = 4.75, $p < 0.05$. None of the remaining 26 effects in the analysis of variance was significant even at the 25% level.

As has been stated above, the truth of the items was not a factor in the analysis of variance design. The design, however, was balanced with respect to the truth of the items. The RT for the true items was 150 ms shorter than for the false items. This difference was only significant when testing with F_1: $F_1(1,18) = 6.47$, $p < 0.05$; $min\ F'(1,12) = 2.00$, $p < 0.25$.

<u>8.1.3 Discussion</u>

A closer inspection of the data suggests an interpretation of the interaction of the conjunctions with the negativity of the second clause. The significant interaction effect consists of the fact that the increase in RT for sentences with a negative second clause over sentences with a positive second clause is 452 ms longer for *unless* sentences than for *if ... then* sentences. This illustrates once again the extra difficulty of the double negative in the *unless not* construction. The RT for the *if ... then* sentences on the other hand depends mainly on the number of negative clauses: the RT for sentences with only a negative first clause is about equal to the RT for sentences with only a negative second clause.

The effect of the longer RT for *unless* sentences than for *if ... then* sentences as well as the effect of the double negative for *unless* constructions (*sad, unless*) have also been found by CLARK and LUCY (1975; CLARK, 1978). In the present experiment, however, the double negativity effect was found only for a negative clause that followed *unless*.

Number of errors and the true-false effect. Some remarks should be made with respect to the number of errors and the RT difference between true and false items. The highest number of errors was found for the complex true items. The four items having the greatest number of errors were actually all true items, constructed with the conjunction *unless* followed by a negative clause. These four items accounted for 41% of the errors in the whole experiment. This might be explained by bias of the subjects to judge a sentence as false if it is very complex. Indeed, a very complex sentence may seem odd to the subject and therefore be judged as false. Partial evidence for this assumption comes from an experiment that was administered to the same subjects immediately after the present experiment. The same items have been presented a second time but now with the instruction to judge whether the sentence sounds odd or not. There appeared to be a strong relation between the complexity of the sentences and the judged oddity. For example, the *unless* items followed by a negative clause were on the average judged more odd than the other sentences: Wilcoxon matched-pairs signed-ranks $z = 2.94$; $p < 0.01$. The present hypothesis is that the more complex a sentence, the more odd it sounds and the more likely the answer "false" will be given. From this hypothesis one would expect that the number of errors for true sentences exceeds the number of errors for false sentences, only if the sentences are complex. This is exactly what is observed. The number of errors for complex true and complex false sentences - i.e., sentences with *unless* followed by a negative clause - is 60 and 21, respectively. The number of errors for the other true and false sentences is 31 and 36, respectively. This interaction is highly significant: $\chi^2(1) = 11.98$, $p < 0.001$. Another confirmation of the present hypothesis comes from the RTs for the most complex true items: the inference sentences expressed with *unless* and two negative clauses. The average RT for incorrect answers is 4481 ms; the average RT for correct answers is 6435 ms. This difference is significant: Wilcoxon matched-pairs signed-ranks $p < 0.01$. This difference is the more remarkable because the RT for incorrect items was on the average about 600 ms longer than the RT for correct answers. The explanation is that subjects, having analyzed complex sentences to a certain point, answer "false"; the more complex the sentence, the stronger this bias. This results in the shorter RT for incorrect answers than for correct answers if the complex sentence is a true sentence. In the case of a complex false sentence, this bias shortens the RT for the correct answer. Accordingly, the answer for the most complex false sentences is deflated by the bias to respond "false" to complex sentences. Consequently it seems advisable to test the true-false effect for all the items except those for which the bias to respond "false" is supposedly strong, the *unless not* sentences expressing an inference relation, where the true-false effect is indeed reversed. Apart from these items, the RT for true items is 235 ms shorter than for false items: $F_1(1,18) = 15.19$, $p < 0.01$; $min\ F'(1,16) = 6.67$ $p < 0.05$. Although the present hypothesis deserves further study, it seems sound enough to consider the observed true-false difference in the present experiment as a reliable difference.

Description of the process. The results can be presented in terms of a process model in which the differentiating operations correspond to observed differences between the RTs to different items (Fig. 8.1). The model essentially gives a description of the coding processes for conditional sentences. These coding processes consist of transformations of the linguistic input into cognitive structures. These cognitive structures are then compared with retrieved knowledge of the facts.

The first clause is coded; a negation requires extra coding time. In line with verification models of CLARK and CHASE (1972) and TRABASSO (1972), one can argue that a negation is coded as an embedding *it is false that* clause. The same process is repeated for the second clause. The conditional conjuncti

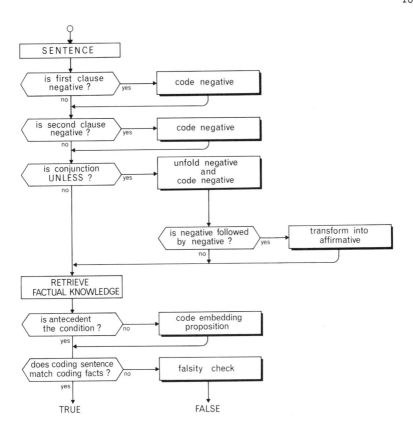

Fig. 8.1. Model for the processing of conditional sentences
in Experiment IV

is transformed into an underlying category for conditionality. The coding of
the conjunction *unless* is somewhat more complicated than the coding of the
conjunction *if ... then*. Only this extra difficulty is represented in the
model. It might be subdivided into two processes. First, the negativity of
unless is made explicit, and then the negation is coded. If in the sentence
unless is followed by a negation, the code of the second clause contains by
now two consecutive negations. The extra processing time for sentences with a
double negative can be accounted for by the operation that transforms two
embedding *it is false that* clauses into one embedding *it is true that* clause.
In other words the two negatives cancel each other.

The sentence code, apart from the negations if any, might at this stage be represented as pRq or $p \to q$, where p and q are the propositions and R or $\to$ indicates the conceptual notion of conditionality. The proposition p is the antecedent: the proposition that occurred after the conjunction in the sentence; q is the consequent, i.e., the other proposition in the sentence. In order to understand the sentence, it must be related to a representation of a conditional relation retrieved from factual knowledge. One might argue that this representation will be in the form of a condition-relation-consequence, i.e., the underlying propositions are appropriately labeled as condition and consequence. It is assumed that this representation is as congruent as possible to the representation towards which the sentence has been transformed. Therefore, the condition and the consequence to be retrieved will be in positive or negative form, depending on the coding of the sentence. The only restriction on the congruence is that the retrieved relations must be true. To summarize, the way in which the sentence is coded will determine the way in which the retrieved information is coded.

How should one account for the longer RT in verifying inference relations than in verifying condition-consequence relations? It might be argued that knowledge on a conditional relation is coded as a condition-relation-consequence configuration. Consequently, in understanding a conditional sentence one has to identify which clause is the condition and which one is the consequence. It has been explained earlier that inference relations are incongruent in the sense that the information that is conceptually the consequence is expressed as the condition as far as the structure of the sentence is concerned. Accordingly, one may argue that the identification or process of search for the condition starts with the antecedent or condition in the sentence, i.e. with the clause that follows the conjunction. The search process for the consequence starts with the consequent, i.e., with the other clause. This search process is essentially a matching process of the coded sentence with retrieved knowledge about the conditional relation. Thus, the antecedent of the sentence is compared to the information that is conceptually the condition. If the antecedent is not, from a conceptual point of view, the condition, then the consequent must be interpreted as the condition and the antecedent as the consequence. The embedding proposition of the inference relation is then coded. This is necessary in order to account for the fact that subjects distinguish between inference relations and condition-consequence relations (Experiments II and III). To summarize, an inference sentence *if q then p* is coded just like the corresponding condition-consequence sentence (*if p then q*) but within the embedding proposition *from q one can infer p, because (if p then q)* as has be discussed earlier. In this way, the two clauses of a conditional sentence, whether an inference relation or a condition-consequence relation, are appropriately coded as condition and consequence. This operation completes the interpretation of the sentence.

One might propose an alternative explanation for the difference between condition-consequence relations and inference relations, assuming that an inference sentence is coded in a form other than a condition-consequence relation. Knowledge about conditional relations however, is assumed again to be coded in a condition-relation-consequence format. If the sentence expresses an inference relation, one should retrieve from this condition-relation-consequence structure an inference relation that matches the coded sentence. The assumption in this explanation is that the retrieval of a condition-consequence relation if the sentence is a condition-consequence relation is easier than the retrieval of an inference relation if the sentence is an inference relation. In the light of evidence to be discussed later, this assumption does not seem to be very plausible.

According to the model up to this point, the clauses of the sentences are coded as condition and consequence, respectively. Both *if ... then* and *unless* sentences are represented in terms of the same underlying notion of conditionality. This representation of the conditional sentence has to be compared with a representation of a conditional relation retrieved from factual knowledge in order to determine the truth of the sentence.

It follows from the characteristics of the coding stages that the only possible difference in the representation of the sentence and the representation of the retrieved information - apart from the embedding proposition for inference relations - consists in the positive or negative character of the condition and the consequence in the two representations. Thus, the comparison stage consists of a matching process. It is determined whether the conditions in the two representations have the same value (positive or negative) and whether the consequences in the two representations have the same value. It has been stressed that the representation of the retrieved information depends on the representation of the sentence. Consequently, there is no mismatch for true sentences, and there is one and only one mismatch for false sentences. This may be illustrated by an example. According to the usual experience of the subjects, knowledge about the shining of the sun and the warmth of the weather may be retrieved in a form such as *sun shining → warm* or *sun not shining → not warm*. The way the knowledge about the sun and warmth is coded is exactly the way the true sentences are coded in the model, so there is no mismatch. The false sentences are coded either as *sun not shining → warm* or as *sun shining → not warm*. Whatever the representation of the retrieved information is, there is always one and only one mismatch. A mismatch requires some extra operation. The subject has to change his initial assumption that the sentence is true into the conclusion that the sentence is false. Alternatively one may argue that the subject checks whether the answer "false" is correct before he executes this answer. These points will be discussed later. Finally the answer is executed.

The processes in the model have been described in an additive way. As has been pointed out earlier, there were no interactions in the analysis of variance between the factors of the model. Similarly, the true-false factor did not interact with any of these factors with the exception that the RT for the most complex false sentences was shorter than the RT for the comparable true sentences; this reversal and a possible interpretation were discussed above. Thus, the operations in the model that differentiate between the items may be considered as additive.

Time estimates have been obtained for the different operations by specifying, for each item type, which operations are involved. Initially this has been done for the 16 items of Table 8.1, where the RT has been averaged over groups of subjects and consequently over the true and false items. The coding of a negation in the first and second clause is 636 and 571 ms, respectively. The extra coding of *unless* over *if ... then* requires 865 ms. The processing of a double negation requires 452 ms. This time increment is, of course, identical to the one mentioned in the discussion about the interaction of the conjunction and clause negativity. Because the double negation occurs in one-half of the *unless* sentences and does not occur in the *if ... then* sentences, the *unless* sentences require on the average 865 + 1/2 x 452 = 1091 ms more than the *if ... then* sentences. This is, of course, exactly the RT difference between *unless* and *if ... then* sentences found in the analysis of variance. The check that the condition is mentioned in the consequent of the sentence and the coding of the embedding proposition require 286 ms. This is the difference corresponding to the main effect inference vs condition-consequence relation in the analysis of variance. The estimate of the base time is 2398 ms.

How well does the model account for the data? Based on this model and the time estimates of the different operations in the model, one can reconstruct the RTs for the items. The coding of a negation was treated as one parameter with the value 604 ms, the average of the coding time for a negation in the first clause and in the second clause. The Pearson correlation with the observed RTs is 0.98.

The items in the present experiment can be considered as a set of 32 different item types by differentiating the items according to the true-false distinction. It should be remembered that this true-false distinction for each of the 16 item types is confounded with the groups of subjects. Therefore, it seems advisable, when introducing true-false as a parameter of the model, to make different estimates of the base time for each group of subjects. The values of the parameters discussed above remain the same. The operation involved in the comparison stage requires 150 ms. The base time for the two groups of subjects is 2561 and 2087 ms, respectively. The Pearson correlation coefficient for the 32 items is 0.96.

In order to get an idea of the reliability of the data, a split-half correlation over the items has been computed by dividing the subjects arbitrarily into two groups of 10 subjects each. This product moment correlation was 0.90.

The present model is in its global organization very similar to the verification models of CLARK and CHASE (CLARK and CHASE, 1972; CHASE and CLARK, 1972) and TRABASSO (TRABASSO et al., 1971; TRABASSO, 1972). In the verification of a sentence against, e.g., a picture, these authors specify a model consisting of four stages: the coding of the sentence, the coding of a picture, the comparison of the two codes, and the execution of the answer. These are essentially the same as the stages in the present model.

Representation of retrieved information. A few remarks should be made with respect to the retrieval of factual knowledge. It has been assumed in the model that the way the sentence is coded determines the way the retrieved information is coded. The reason is that the two representations must be compared; therefore, they should be as comparable as possible. This principle is similar to the principle put forward by CLARK (1974); CLARK and CHASE (1972), and CLARK et al. (1973) when discussing the coding of visual information. In the latter studies it is the coding of visual information that is determined by the form of the sentence describing that information. Although a picture normally is coded in a positive form, they demonstrated that a picture is interpreted in a negative form if it is preceded by a negative sentence describing the picture. In another experiment it was demonstrated that the same dot-pattern consisting of 14 black dots and two red dots is coded in terms of the smaller or larger subset, depending on whether the preceding sentence describing the pattern contained the quantifier *minority* or *few*, respectively (JUST and CARPENTER, 1971).

Because the form of the information to be retrieved depends on the form of the sentence, negative information will be retrieved when a negative sentence is presented. For example, if the sentence to be verified is *if the sun is not shining, it is not warm,* the retrieved information might be represented as *not sun → not warm* instead of *sun → warm,* which is the representation of the retrieved information in case of a positive sentence. If one were not to assume this optional retrieval of negative information, one would expect a difference in the wrong direction between the two kinds of sentence topics. Sentences with the first kind of topic have been defined earlier as sentences that are true either if both clauses are positive or if both clauses are negative, e.g., *if the sun is shining, it is warm.* Sentences with the second kind of topic are true if one and only one of the clauses is negative, e.g., *if John is ill, he is not going to his work.* In the latter case the information to be retrieved from factual knowledge contains one negative proposition. If for the former kind of sentences the information to be retrieved would always be in positive form, the number of mismatches in the comparison stage for the first kind of sentences should be greater than for the second kind of sentences. Consequently, one would expect the RT for the first kind of sentence to be longer than for the second kind of sentence. If anything, the results are just the reverse: 3627 and 3755 ms for the first and second kinds of sentences, respectively.

The assumption about the optional form of the information to be retrieved is in complete agreement with the conclusion of the first experiment, that conditional relations are interpreted as biconditionals. Actually, the information to be retrieved is for the first kind of sentence either *sun → warm* or *not sun → not warm.* For the second kind of sentence it is either *ill → not working* or *not ill → working.* That either form may be retrieved, depending on the sentence, means precisely that conditional relations are interpreted as biconditional relations. Moreover, the data on true and false sentences confirm this biconditional interpretation. Suppose that the sentences were interpreted as conditionals: the information to be retrieved would be only *ill → not working* and not *not ill → working* if the sentences deal with illness and working; *sun → warm* and not *not sun → not warm* if the sentences deal with the temperature and the shining of the sun. This would result in an average of one and only one mismatch for true sentences as well as for false sentences and one would expect the RT for true and false sentences to be equal, which is contrary to the results.

A final point should be discussed with respect to the retrieval of negative information. Does the retrieval of negative information require extra time? This question does not refer to the difference in processing between positive and negative information in general. It should be remembered that in the present task negative information is retrieved when the sentence is coded in negative form. The question stated more completely is: does the retrieval of negative information, initiated by a negative sentence coding, require more time than the retrieval of positive information, initiated by a positive sentence coding? The crucial comparison is whether the RT difference for sentences like *if the sun is shining, it is warm* and *if the sun is not shining, it is not warm* is greater than the RT difference between *if John is ill, he is going to his work* and *if John is not ill, he is not going to his work*. According to the model, the first two sentences differ with respect to the coding of negative clauses as well as with respect to the retrieval of negative information. The sentences of the latter pair differ only with respect to the coding of negative clauses. This comparison can be generalized so as to include a similar estimate of the retrieval time for negative information for *unless* sentences. Because no assumption is made as to whether positive or negative information is retrieved in the case of sentences which are coded with only one negative as, e.g., *if the sun is not shining, it is warm*, the present comparison concerns only one-half of the items in the experiment. The retrieval time for negative information did not differ from the retrieval time for positive information. The difference was actually a nonsignificant 245 ms in the wrong direction, i.e., a shorter time was found for the retrieval of negative information.

The conclusion is that the retrieval of negative information does not require more time than the retrieval of positive information according to the model. What does this result mean? First, one could conclude that the model is incorrect as far as its coding stage is concerned. The retrieval of negative information is required in the present model in case, e.g., both clauses are coded as negatives. Thus, one should change the coding processes: a sentence with two negatives, e.g., *if the sun is not shining, it is not warm* is coded in positive form: *if the sun is shining, it is warm*. The two negatives cancel each other. This process is similar to that proposed in the optional recoding model of TRABASSO (1972). The result is that no negative information has to be retrieved. The extra time for sentences with two negative clauses is attributed here to the transformation or recoding of two negative clauses into two positive clauses. The only problem with this explanation, however, is one of parsimony. The recoding operation replaces the coding processes of negative sentences only when both are negative. If only one clause is a negative, the coding of that negation is required. Thus, this explanation adds a new operation to the model without removing one.

The alternative interpretation keeps the model as it is. This interpretation assumes that the retrieval of negative information when the retrieval process is directed by a negative sentence representation does not require more time than the retrieval of positive information when the retrieval process is directed by a positive sentence representation. This interpretation argues that this result is another instance of the influence of context on information processing. A plausible context will greatly reduce the difficulty of a negation (WASON, 1965). The negation of an exceptional item will be easier then the negation of an unexceptional item. In terms of WASON and JOHNSON-LAIRD (1972, p.32) "it was evidently easier to negate the exceptional item in terms of the property which makes it an exception than to negate an unexceptional item in terms of the property of the exceptional item". Another example is provided by research on marked and unmarked adjectives. Marked terms are generally more diffcult to process than unmarked terms. This difference disappears, however, when the feature on which the terms differ is stressed by the context (Part I). Similarly, an asymmetry in the processing of male and female kinship terms disappears when the sex of the terms is stressed by the context (Part III). The asymmetry between marked and unmarked words as well as between positive and negative polarity items has been discussed in terms of foreground and background information (NOORDMAN, 1978). The context can eliminate the difference in foreground and background by stressing the relevant information.

True-false effect. Having discussed the coding stages, some remarks should be made with respect to the comparison stage. The true-false difference might be accounted for in two ways. The first one is conform to the model of CLARK and CHASE (1972). The principle underlying the comparison stage in their model is: the sentence is true unless a mismatch is found. A mismatch requires extra processing time: the truth index has to be reversed from true, which is the initial assumption, to false. These kinds of models are called truth index models. The other way to account for the true-false difference is more in line with the verification model of NOORDMAN-VONK (1979). A sentence is false not just if it is not true, but only if positive evidence is obtained for its falsity. That is, subjects try to verify the falsity of the sentence. There is a kind of double check on whether the answer "false" is correct. These kinds of models may be called verification-falsification models. When a subject has to decide whether both *oak* and *sparrow* belong to one of the categories *tree, flower, bird, insect,* he will retrieve the categories of both concepts in order to see whether they match. Having found a mismatch, the process goes on to justify this mismatch. The subject will verify the difference between the two concepts. The difference consists in the fact that one concept is a plant and the other one is an animal.

The results in the present experiment can be accounted for in a similar way. Having found a mismatch between retrieved information and sentence representation, the subject sets out to justify, in a kind of double check, that the conclusion "false" is the correct conclusion. It is as if the subject concludes: "the sentence *if it is raining, the streets are not wet* is false because rain would imply that the streets are wet. Thus, the consequence *not wet* is false because *wet* is true". This was indicated in the model by the operation: falsity check.

From a logical point of view, the operation "falsity check" is superfluous. A highly practiced subject may be able to skip that check. This would result in an equal RT for true and false matches. According to the truth index model, however, the operation: "change truth index" is necessary for obtaining the answer. It is the state of the truth index at the end of the matching process which is produced as the answer. Consequently, the RT for true matches should be shorter than for false matches. TRABASSO et. al. (1971) report an experiment with a highly practiced subject in which no effect was found for the changes of the truth index. This evidence supports the present theory on falsification that postulates an extra check when a mismatch is found. The present theory may not be interpreted to imply that the RT for false sentences is necessarily longer than for true sentences. The theory specifies a difference in RT on the micro level of the matching processes: a mismatch generally requires an extra falsification procedure. Therefore, if in the verification of a true sentence two mismatches occur, the RT will be longer than for the verification of a false sentence in which only one mismatch occurs. This is what CLARK and CHASE found for true negative and false negative sentences.

8.1.4 Conclusion

The present model accounts for the verification of conditional sentences, as studied in Experiment IV. The model can be conceived of as a summary of the results of the previous experiments as well: conditional sentences are interpreted predominantly as biconditional sentences; they differ in difficulty depending on the conjunction that is used and depending on whether they express a condition-consequence relation or an inference relation. Accordingly, the factors that consitute the present model can account for the processing of conditional sentences in a variety of tasks. One should, however, not wrongly generalize the model. The results of the present experiments may not be interpreted to imply that there is only one underlying representation and only one process model for conditional sentences. All the sentences used in the present experiments have a word-to-world direction of fit and not a world-to-word direction of fit, to use SEARLE's (1976) terminology. The sentences were descriptions of the contingency of one event or state on another event or state. They were neutral with respect to the assumptions and expectations of the listener and speaker. Sentences whose aim it is to influence the behavior of the hearer such as promises, threats, and warnings (FILLENBAUM, 1974, 1975, 1976) were not included in the present material. It is quite possible that under certain circumstances *unless* sentences are more appropriate and easier to process than *if ... then* sentences. Results of an unpublished experiment of Noordman are relevant in this respect. The intention of the listener to satisfy the condition expressed in a conditional sentence and the expectation of the speaker that the condition will be satisfied is less strong for *unless* sentences than for *if ... then* sentences. *Unless* sentences express a greater pressure of the speaker on the listener to fulfill the condition than *if ... then* sentences. If the context satisfies these "conditions of use" for *unless* sentences, *unless* sentences are more appropriate and might be easier to process than *if ... then* sentences.

Part III   Foreground and Background Information in Inferential Processes

Every meaningful message contains new information and old information, foreground information and background information. Foreground information is the explicitly communicated information; background information is supposed to be known by the speaker and the listener. Background information is more likely presupposed to be true and less likely to be affected by a negation than foreground information. This foreground-background distinction has been studied with respect to kinship terms. In the first experiments kinship terms were used in negative sentences. The results indicated that the gender is background information. There apppeared to be an asymmetry in this respect between some male and female terms: the feature male behaves like a presupposition of a higher order than the feature female. The same asymmetry has been found in other experiments where subjects had to make a decision with respect to gender and generation. It appeared that the asymmetry could be influenced by manipulating foreground and background information, as was expected. The asymmetry between kinship terms is very similar to the asymmetry between unmarked and marked adjectives. The conclusion is that the foreground-background distinction offers a very good description for a variety of phenomena in inference processes.

Introduction

Every meaningful message contains new information, or at least information meant by the speaker to be new for the listener, embedded in old information. Every message aims at communicating something new. The phrase *two and two is four* would be meaningless at this point, because it contains only old information, and nothing new is communicated. On the other hand, a sentence that contains only new information, e.g., *suddenly he got extremely angry* cannot be understood, it cannot be assimilated to previous knowledge. The quite normal sentence *I met your brother yesterday* contains as new information that a particular meeting has taken place at a particular moment. There is also old information: knowledge shared by the speaker and listener which is presupposed to be true. That presupposed information in this case is, among others: the listener has a brother. A linguist who has studied verbal communication and semantics in the framework of old and new information is CHAFE (1970, 1972). Related distinctions are topic and comment, given and new, theme and rheme (HALLIDAY, 1967, 1970), presupposition and focus (CHOMSKY, 1971).

The psychological implications of new and old information have especially been studied by CLARK (1973b; CLARK and HAVILAND, 1977). He has developed a theory on communication and comprehension in terms of the given-new contract, elaborating upon GRICE's cooperative principle (1967). According to CLARK, the speaker is cooperative if he communicates information he thinks the listener already knows as given information, and information he thinks the listener does not yet know as new information. He can do this by using a certain syntactic construction or a certain stress pattern. The listener divides incoming information into given and new information, he then searches memory for a unique antecedent that matches the given information; the new information is integrated into memory by attaching it to that unique antecedent. HAVILAND and CLARK (1974) demonstrated that the comprehension of sentences requires more time if the unique antecedent that matches the given information is not directly available than when it is directly available. If the antecedent is not available, the listener has to construct the antecedent by using strategies such as adding information, bridging or reconstituting the information. They investigated the comprehension of sentences with a definite noun phrase and sentences with the adverbs *either*, *again*, *too*, and *still*. These sentences presuppose some particular information. These presuppositions constitute the given information. The comprehension of sequences of senten- ces such as *Mary got some picnic supplies out of the car. The beer was warm* required more time than the comprehension of *Mary got some beer out of the car. The beer was warm*. In the former case a "bridging" operation is requir- ed in order to find the antecedent for the definite noun phrase, which iden- tifies the given information.

Related to the notions of given and new information are the notions of presupposition and assertion. The notion of presupposition of a sentence is generally defined as the expression of those conditions that must be true for the sentence to make sense (FREGE, 1892; KEENAN, 1971; LANGENDOEN and SAVIN, 1971). The standard test for the claim that a certain proposition is the presupposition of a sentence is to see whether it is preserved under negation (FRASER, 1971; HORN, 1969; LAKOFF, 1972). The negation in the sen- tence *I did not meet your brother yesterday* does not affect the old infor- mation that you have a brother. To cite an example of AUSTIN: the sentences: *John's children are bald* and *John's children are not bald* only make sense when John has children. *John has children* is the presupposition of *John's children are bald*. "To talk about those children or to refer to them pre- supposes that they exist" (AUSTIN, 1963). Another illustration of a presuppo- sition is the sentence: *The present King of France is bald*. This sentence does not make sense; it is neither true nor false, because there is no pre- sent King of France. *There is a King of France* is the presupposition of the sentence and that presupposition is violated. This notion of presupposition is called logical presupposition. It is defined ultimately on the relation between base structures and the world (KEENAN, 1971).

The notion of presupposition can be defined in a somewhat different way: with respect to the beliefs of the listener and speaker. The test for the claim that a certain proposition is a presupposition of a sentence is to see whether it is preserved under negation of the sentence as it is understood by the listener and speaker. In this case the presupposition of a sentence is not the proposition that logically has to be true in order for the senten- ce to have a truth value, but the proposition that actually is considered to be true. In this study the notion of presupposition is used in the latter, pragmatic way. It is in this sense also that MILLER (1969) uses the notion of presupposition. He discusses the implications of a negation in a predicate nominal sentence, e.g., *Leslie is not a mother*. It is an empirical question to determine the implications of a negation, as MILLER argues. He suggests that the sentence *X is not a mother* implies that X is a woman and denies that X is a parent: *woman* is the presupposition of *mother*, because it is not affected by the negation; *parent*, which is negated with respect to X, is called the assertion. Another observation made by MILLER concerns the organization of the subjective lexicon in terms of presuppositions and assertions. The presupposition of a noun, e.g., of the noun *mother*, can be analyzed itself in terms of presupposition and assertion. The sentence *X is not a woman* denies that X is female and implies that X is a person: *female* is the assertion of *woman* and a presupposition of *mother; person* is a presupposition of *woman* and a presupposition of *mother*. This organization of the subjective lexicon will be referred to when discussing the notion of higher order presupposition.

The empirical question raised by MILLER, regarding the implications of a negation in a predicate nominal sentence, will be discussed in this study for some sentences involving a kinship term. In particular the hypothesis that the gender is a presupposition of the kinship terms will be tested.

It is clear that the notion of presupposition as used in this study is different from the logical notion. The sentence *Leslie is not a mother* does not, from a logical point of view, necessarily presuppose that Leslie is fefemale. Leslie could be a man: the presupposition can be negated. What is claimed however, is that the speaker and the listener of the sentence *Leslie is not a mother* presuppose or believe that Leslie is a woman. Consequently, if the sentence *Leslie is not a mother* is used in a context that necessitates interpreting Leslie as a man, the listener will have difficulty in arriving at the correct interpretation of the sentence. The listener wrongly presupposes that Leslie is female. That presupposition has to be denied before the correct interpretation can be made. This will take some time, if it can be done at all.

The point to be made is that only some information is explicitly communicated in the sentence, whereas other information is tacitly assumed to be true. The sentences *X is not a painter* and *X is a painter* explicitly communicate something about the profession of X. Not explicitly communicated is, e.g., that X is living and human. That information is assumed to be true in both sentences; it is not easily available for a negation: *X is not a painter but a stone* sounds strange to say the least. The explicitly communicated information will be called foreground information. Information which is not explicitly communicated but which is presupposed by the speaker and listener is called background information. Thus, the above-discussed given information and presupositions might be called background information. As has been pointed out above, the present study deals with pragmatic presuppositions, defined with respect to the beliefs and the expectations of the listener and speaker. Accordingly, the notion of background information will be restricted to this kind of presupposition.

Background information is normally assumed to be true, just as given information. HORNBY (1974) demonstrated that people assume that given information is true and attempt to verify new information. The notion of background information can be considered as a pragmatic extension of given information. It differs from given information in the sense that background information is not identified as given in the sentence, but it is defined with respect to pragmatic factors such as beliefs and expectations. The present experiments will illustrate some differences between given information and background information.

The aim of the study is to demonstrate the role of foreground and background information in simple inference tasks. Not all information is equally likely to be background information. Some factors will be discussed that determine what information is likely to be foreground information and what information is likely to be background information.

Chapter 9   Presupposed or Background Information

In the first experiments to be reported, very simple problem solving tasks
have been used, each of which involves a negative sentence. The task is such
that in order to arrive at the conclusion, a particular proposition has to
be negated. It is assumed that the solution of these tasks is straightfor-
ward if a subject can negate that proposition. If many subjects are unable
to solve the task, this will indicate that that proposition is wrongly presupposed to be true. The existence of such presuppositions is inferred from
the difficulty of the task. A task is considered to be difficult when it can
hardly be solved or when it takes a relatively long time to solve it as compared to other tasks with which it is matched in all relevant aspects.

9.1 Experiment I[1]

The starting point of this experiment was the following well-known riddle.
"Two Indians, a tall one and a short one, were sitting on a fence; the shorter one was the son of the taller one; the taller one was not the father of
the shorter one. How is that possible?" Most people have great difficulty in
solving this problem. They are not able to deny the masculinity of the tall
Indian. The negation in *the taller one is not the father of the shorter one*
apparently does not affect the feature male. This indicates that male is a
presupposition of father which agrees with Miller's analysis.

It could be argued, however, that the difficulty of the problem rests not
only in the presuppositional structure of the kinship term but also in other
factors. Indians are normally assumed to be male Indians. Thus, an implication of the first sentence might be that the two persons are male, which is
not true. However, the negation in the sentence *the taller one is not the*

---

[1] The research reported in this experiment has been done in collaboration
with Dr. W.J.M. Levelt.

father of the shorter one does not change the belief of the listener that the taller one is male. So the conclusion remains the same: in this context *male* is a presupposition of *father*. Anyhow, the effect of the word *Indians* can be eliminated by constructing the problem in the form: *A is the son of B, B is not the father of A*. The possibility that *A* and *B* are interpreted as male persons because of the use of initials can be rejected experimentally, as will appear later. Another factor contributing to the difficulty of the problems might be the presence of kinship terms of the same sex in both sentences. When kinship terms contrasting on the gender component are used in the sentences, the attention of the listener might be focused on the decisive feature gender. Consequently, it is less likely that the gender is background information and consequently more likely that the gender will be affected by the negation. If this is correct, the following problem should be much easier: *A is the daughter of B, B is not the father of A*. It is assumed that the context determines what information is background and foreground information. Similar remarks can be made with respect to the problem *A is the daughter of B, B is not the mother of A* and *A is the son of B, B is not the mother of A*. Two more riddles have been used in the experiment: *A is the child of B, B is not the father of A* and *A is the child of B, B is not the mother of A*. There is no similarity or dissimilarity of the sex of the two kinship terms in these items. The difficulty of these items is therefore expected to be intermediate between the same-sex items and the opposite-sex items.

9.1.1 Method

Material. The six items used in this experiment are presented in Table 9.1.

Procedure. Because of the riddle character of the items, each subject was given only one item. Each item was presented to 17 subjects. The subjects were run individually. A subject was told that he had to solve a riddle. An item, followed by the question *how is that possible,* was presented auditively. The time was measured from the end of the presentation of the question until the subject gave the answer. If the subject did not give the answer within 120 s, he was considered to be unable to solve the problem, and the experimenter stopped the session.

Subjects. The subjects were male and female psychology students who volunteered in the experiment.

Table 9.1. Items, median latencies [s], and number of subjects who gave the correct answer in Experiment I

Item	Median latency	Number correct
1 A is the son of B B is not the father of A	[a]	2
2 A is the daughter of B B is not the father of A	68	9
3 A is the child of B B is not the father of A	24	16
4 A is the daughter of B B is not the mother of A	26	12
5 A is the son of B B is not the mother of A	11	17
6 A is the child of B B is not the mother of A	10	14

Note: n = 17 per item.

[a] For absence of median see text.

9.1.2 Results

The experimental data are the latencies and the number of errors. The latencies have been analyzed with the Mann-Whitney-U test. To subjects who gave an incorrect answer or no answer at all, the highest possible rank was attributed in these tests. The median latency and the number of errors for each item are presented in Table 9.1. The median latency for item 1 is not reported. Because that item has not been solved by more than one-half of the subjects, the median cannot be computed in a nonarbitrary way. The gender of the subjects did not affect the latencies; male and female subjects reacted in th same way.

The results confirm the predictions with respect to the difficulty of the problems. A large number of subjects could not solve their problem. If they were able to solve the problems, it took a relatively long time. Apparently, the subjects have difficulty in negating the sex component. The gender is a presupposition or background information. The analysis of the errors confirms this conclusion: *stepfather* was a frequent reaction in item 1 and *stepmother* in item 4.

Items with kinship terms of a different sex are easier than items with kinship terms of the same sex: $z = 2.77$, $p < 0.01$. Accordingly, in the former items where the kinship terms contrast on the gender component, the gender is less likely to be background information and more available for negation than in the same-sex items. Three out of the four individual comparisons that can be made with respect to this hypothesis have been confirmed: the item *son, not father* is more difficult than the item *daughter, not father*: $z = 2.34$, $p < 0.05$; *daughter, not mother* is more difficult than *son, not mother*: $z = 2.49$, $p < 0.05$; *son, not father* is more difficult than *son, not mother*: $z = 4.88$, $p < 0.001$; but *daughter, not mother* is not more difficult than *daughter, not father*. This deviant comparison will be discussed below.

Contrary to expectation, the difficulty of the items with the term *child* is not intermediate between the difficulty of the same-sex items and the opposite-sex items. When the second sentence is *not mother*, the item containing *child* in the first sentence does not differ from the items with *son* and *daughter*: $z = 0.65$, $p > 0.50$; $z = 1.66$, $0.05 < p < 0.10$, respectively. When the second sentence is *not father*, the item with *child* is easier than the items with *son* and *daughter*: $z = 4.33$, $p < 0.001$; $z = 2.63$, $p < 0.01$, respectively. This interaction might indicate a closer relation between *child* and *mother* than between *child* and *father*.

There is an additional significant result. The items with *B is not the father of A* are more difficult than the items with *B is not the mother of A*: $z = 4.21$, $p < 0.001$. Apparently, it is easier to conclude from *B is not the mother* that *B* is the father than from *B is not the father* that *B* is the mother. One could say that the masculinity of *father* is more strongly presupposed or background information than the femininity of *mother*. This male-female asymmetry will be discussed in Chap. 10. This asymmetry accounts for the one deviant comparison mentioned above: the item *daughter, not mother* is not more difficult than the item *daughter, not father*. The two factors that determine the difficulty of the problems are antagonistic: the difficulty of two kinship terms of the same sex is counteracted by the male-female asymmetry.

The present experiment illustrates the characteristics of background information with respect to which it differs from given information. First, background information is not identified as given in the sentence; it is the information which is presupposed to be given. Second, "background" in this

presupposed information is a matter of degree as is indicated by the male-
female asymmetry: some information is more strongly expected to be true than
other information. Background information can vary in strength just as beliefs and expectations with respect to which background information is defined.

The conclusion so far is that the gender is the background information of
the kinship terms *father* and *mother* in these problems. It is plausible then
that the foreground information is parenthood. A negation affects the foreground information. Consequently, it is expected that the meaning component
parenthood is most likely to be affected by a negation. It is clear that this
prediction rests on the following principle: when a sentence is negated, the
negation, as a rule, affects only one meaning component of that sentence. This
principle will be called the principle of minimal negation. Evidence for this
principle has been found in several unpublished experiments on negation by
Noordman and Levelt. Moreover, the incorrect answers in the previous experiment (*stepfather* and *stepmother*) confirm that only the parenthood and not the
gender is negated.

The principle of minimal negation and the prediction that the meaning
component parenthood is most likely to be affected by the negation have been
tested in two problems in which both the gender component and the parenthood
component can be negated.

9.2 Experiment II

The first problem is: *A is the father of B, A is the grandfather of C, B is
not the father of C, what could B be of C?* There are three possible answers:
mother, uncle, and *aunt. Mother* differs from *father* with respect to gender;
uncle differs from *father* with respect to parenthood; *aunt* differs from *father* with respect to both meaning components. If, according to the principle
of minimal negation, only one meaning component is changed, and if, according
to the foreground-background hypothesis, gender is the background information
then parenthood will be negated and the most frequent answer will be *uncle.*
A similar prediction can be made with respect to the problem: *A is the mother
of B, A is the grandmother of C, B is not the mother of C, what could B be
of C?* Again there are three possible answers: *father, aunt,* and *uncle.* If
parenthood is the foreground information and gender the background information, the most frequent answer will be *aunt.* Based on the results of Experiment I, however, one should expect that the gender is not as difficult to

negate for the *mother-grandmother* problem as for the *father-grandfather* problem.

9.2.1 Method

The two items described above have been presented on cards[2]. There were 80 subjects in the experiment: 40 subjects for each problem. The experiment was balanced with respect to the sex of the experimenter and of the subjects.

9.2.2 Results

The sex of the experimenter and of the subject had no effect. The answers and their frequencies are presented in Table 9.2. The results of the *father-grandfather* problem confirm the predictions. No subject gave the correct answer *aunt*, which confirms the principle of minimal negation: the negation affects only one meaning component. There is a strong tendency to negate the parenthood component. The frequency of the answer *uncle* is greater than the frequency of the answer *mother*. The total number of gender preserving answers is greater than the number of gender changing answers: $\chi^2(1) = 13.56$, $p < 0.001$. The conclusion is that the gender is the background information and parenthood foreground information

The results with respect to the *mother-grandmother* problem are less dramatic. The total number of gender preserving answers is greater than the number of gender changing answers, but not significantly: $\chi^2(1) = 2.08$, $0.10 < p < 0.20$. In fact, the difference between the gender preserving and the gender changing answers is greater for the *father-grandfather* than for the *mother-grandmother* problem: $\chi^2(1) = 3.02$, $p < 0.05$ one tail. This is in agreement with the observed asymmetry between *father* and *mother* in the previous experiment. Again, the principle of minimal negation has been confirmed: no subject gave the answer *uncle*, which differs on two meaning components from *mother*.

The principle of minimal negation has also been confirmed by data of LEVELT et al. (1978) in a study of verbs of motion. This principle is in complete agreement with the rule of minimal contrast formulated by CLARK (1970b) for word association data. That rule says: "change the sign of one feature, be-

---

[2] The author is indebted to Ms. E. Gijsen, Mr. J. Tijshen, and Mr. R. Van Hout, who conducted the experiment as part of a "doctoraal werkstuk" with Dr. W.J.M. Levelt. For more details, see VAN HOUT and TIJSHEN (1976).

Table 9.2. Answers and their frequency in Experiment II

Problem father-grandfather					
Answers				Meaning component	
correct		incorrect		gender	parenthood
uncle	20	a male term	11	preserved	31	10
mother	8	a female term	0	changed	8	30
aunt	0	child	1	neutral	1	
		no answer	0			

Problem mother-grandmother					
Answers				Meaning component	
correct		incorrect		gender	parenthood
aunt	12	a male term	0	preserved	24	19
father	15	a female term	12	changed	15	20
uncle	0	child	0	no answer	1	1
		no answer	1			

ginning with the bottommost feature", assuming that features can be ordered in a motivated way (p. 276). The most frequent association to *man* is *woman* where only the sex is changed, then *boy* implying a change in the feature adult, and then *girl*, implying a change in both features.

Chapter 10 Differences in Background Information

The results so far demonstrate that gender is background information of the kinship terms. A second result is that the masculinity of *father* is more background information than the femininity of *mother*. In other words, *father* and *mother* are asymmetric with respect to background information. An interesting question is whether there are kinship terms that are more symmetric than *father* and *mother*. According to LYONS (1968), this is the case for *brother* and *sister*: "The fact that there is no superordinate term for the two complementaries *brother* and *sister*, is prima facie evidence that the opposition between the two terms is semantically more important than what they have in common" (p. 479). Consequently, the asymmetry found for *father* and *mother* should not be found for *brother* and *sister*. On the other hand, the results for items with *son* and *daughter* should exhibit the same asymmetry as those for *father* and *mother*.

10.1 Experiment III

The items are presented in Table 10.1. Condition I contains the *not son* and *not daughter* items, e.g., *A is the father of B, B is not the son of A*. Condition II contains the *not brother* and *not sister* items, e.g., *A is the brother of B, B is not the brother of A*.

Assuming again that gender is the background information of these kinship terms, it is predicted that subjects will need a relatively long time to solve these problems, if they can be solved at all. The other prediction is that the *B is not the son* items are more difficult than the *B is not the daughter* items and that there is no difference between the *B is not the brother* items and *B is not the sister* items. In conformance with the results of Experiment I, it is expected that the items with the terms *father son* and *mother daughter* are more difficult than items with the terms *mother son* and *father daughter*.

126

Table 10.1. Items, median latencies [s], and number of correct answers in Experiment III

Item	Median latency	Number correct
Condition I (n = 10 per item)		
1. A is the father of B	a	3
B is not the son of A		
2. A is the mother of B	13	7
B is not the son of A		
3. A is the mother of B	9	7
B is not the daughter of A		
4. A is the father of B	10	9
B is not the daughter of A		
Condition II (n = 12 per item)		
1. A is the brother of B	a	6
B is not the brother of A		
2. A is the sister of B	a	6
B is not the brother of A		
3. A is the sister of B	34	8
B is not the sister of A		
4. A is the brother of B	a	4
B is not the sister of A		

[a] For absence of median, see text.

10.1.1 Method

This experiment is similar to Experiment I, except in some minor respects. The items and the question *how is that possible?* have been presented using a tape recorder. At the end of the presentation of the question a timer was automatically started. The timer was stopped by the subject's response by means of a voice key. Each items in condition I was presented to five male and five female subjects; each item in condition II was presented to six male and six female subjects. Each subject was presented with only one item. The subjects were university students who volunteered in the experiment.

10.1.2 Results

The results are presented in Table 10.1. Again no medians have been reported for items that have been solved by less than one-half of the subjects. The latencies have been analyzed with the Mann-Whitney-U test. The sex of the subjects did not have a differential effect on the latencies.

The results are in agreement with those of Experiment I: subjects have difficulty in denying gender. A large number of subjects could not solve their problem. The gender is the background information in these problems.

The latencies for the items *B is not the son* are longer than for the items *B is not the daughter*: $z = 1.71$; $p < 0.05$ one tail. The masculinity of *son* is more background information than the femininity of *daughter*. On the other hand, the items *B is not the sister* were as difficult as the items *B is not the brother*, as was expected: $z = 0.46$, $p = 0.65$. The gender is equally background information in *brother* and *sister*.

Items with terms of the same sex in condition I were not more difficult than items with terms of different sex: $z = 1.13$; $p = 0.13$ one tail. This lack of difference is mainly due to the relative ease of the item *A is the mother of B, B is not the daughter of A*. Actually, the item *A is the father of B, B is not the son of A* was more difficult than the two items with kinship terms of opposite sex: $z = 2.12$; $p < .05$. This point will be discussed later when discussing the role of the first sentence in the items.

One more remark should be made with respect to the fact that the *B is not the sister* items are as difficult as the *B is not the brother* items. One could claim that the male-female asymmetry found for the terms *father, mother, son,* and *daughter* is due to the use of initials, arguing for example that initials are normally used, e.g., in newspapers, to indicate only male persons, whereas female persons are usually indicated by initials preceded by Mrs. or Miss. This factor can be ruled out, however, because the *B is not the sister* items are as diffcult as the *B is not the brother* items.

The asymmetry between *father* and *mother* and between *son* and *daughter* has been interpreted in the sense that the masculinity of the male terms in these pairs is more background information than the femininity of the female terms in these pairs. Male is background information just as the features, e.g., human, living, concrete. These features are sometimes called higher order presuppositions; they are presuppositions of presuppositions: man presupposes human, human presupposes living, living presupposes concrete. Higher order

128

presuppositions are less vulnerable to a negation than first-order presuppositions. The sentence *this child is not married* is less strange than the sentence *this stone is not married*. By attributing *not married* or *stone*, not only the presupposed information of the feature adult, but also of the features living and human are negated. Another example comes from LAKOFF (1972):

1) *few men have stopped beating their wives*
2) *some men have stopped beating their wives*
3) *some men have beaten their wives*

Sentence 1 presupposes sentence 2; 2 is the first-order presupposition of 1. Sentence 2 presupposes sentence 3; 3 is the second-order presupposition of 1. A first-order presupposition can be suspended, as is demonstrated in 4:

4) *few men have stopped beating their wives,*
   if any at all have

A higher order presupposition cannot be suspended: sentence 5 is not acceptable:

5) *few men have stopped beating their wives,*
   if any have ever beaten them at all

In line with this analysis one could say that in these problems the masculinity of *father* behaves like a presupposition of a higher order than the femininity of *mother*. It is not claimed that masculinity is a presupposition of a higher order than femininity in the sense that masculinity would be a presupposition of a presupposition and femininity not; the claim is that masculinity and femininity behave like presuppositions of different order as far as the effect of a negation is concerned. The negation is less likely to affect the feature male of *father* than the feature female of *mother*. The same remark can be made with respect to the asymmetry between *son* and *daughter*.

Chapter 11   Dependency of Background Information on Context

The difficulty of the riddles discussed in the previous chapters consists in the fact that some information is wrongly assumed to be true. This information is assumed to be given; it functions as background information, it is hardly or not affected by the negation. The discussion of the difficulty of the riddles has focussed on the role of the second, i.e., the negative sentence. The question to be studied in this chapter is: Where does this background information come from? There are, no doubt, cultural factors involved, especially with respect to the observed male-female asymmetry. But also the context will determine which information is old or background and which information is new or foreground. The context for the negative sentence in the riddles is the first, i.e., the affirmative sentence. Thus, the question is to what extent the first sentence creates background information. That the first sentence has an important role in determining the background information is clear from the earlier experiments. Problems in which the gender of the term in the first sentence is the same as the gender of the term in the second sentence are more difficult to solve than problems with kinship terms of different sex. It should be noted, however, that this factor by itself cannot account for the difficulty of the problem. In fact, the item, e.g., *A is the daughter of B, B is not the father of A* was hard to solve and more difficult than all other items, except one, in Experiment I. One-half of the subjects did not even solve this item. Subjects apparently have difficulty in negating the gender in the second sentence even if kinship terms of both sexes occur in the item. A similar conclusion emerges from, e.g., the *brother* and *sister* riddles. Consequently, the second sentence is also important in determining the difficulty of the problems. Whatever the role of the affirmative information in the first sentence may be in creating the background information, the second sentence is not able to negate that information: the negation in *B is not the father of A* hardly affects the masculinity of *father*. Consequently, the conclusion about the foreground and background distinction remains valid: parenthood is foreground information, and gender is background information in these problems.

The present chapter deals with the role of the first sentence. That sentence will probably lead subjects to presuppose certain information. It is assumed that the first sentence is important in determining the strength of the background information.

Two experiments will be reported. In both experiments some information about two persons is given, and the subject has to make an inference about one of the persons. In a sense these experiments are a mirror image of the previous ones. The previous experiments studied the difficulty of denying a meaning component; the difficulty of denying such a meaning component was an indication of presupposed or background information. The following experiments deal with the expectations about the same meaning components. In this case the expectation is an indication of presupposed information. In the first experiment subjects are presented with a sentence for 2 s, e.g., *A is the father of B*. Then, another sentence is presented, e.g., *B is the son of A*, and the subject has to decide whether the second sentence can be true, given the first sentence. The dependent variable is the RT. In the second experiment only one sentence is presented, e.g., *A is the father of B*. But now the subject has to judge what *B* most likely will be. The dependent variable is the frequency of the answers.

11.1 Experiment IV

The aim of this experiment is to investigate to what extent the presupposed or background information in the previous experiments is created by the first sentence. In other words the question is what the expectations of the subject are with respect to *B*, given the first sentence: *A is the ... of B*. Predictions can be based on the previous experiments. Therefore, the results of the previous experiments will be reanalyzed grouping the items on the basis of the first sentence.

For reasons to be explained later, only the kinship terms *father, mother, son, daughter,* and *child* have been used in this experiment. Items with first sentence *A is the son of B* were more difficult when the second sentence was *B is not the father of A* than when the second sentence was *B is not the mother of A*: Mann-Whitney-U test $z = 4.88$, $p < 0.001$. A similar result is found for items with *A is the father of B* as the first sentence: Mann-Whitney-U test $z = 2.23$, $p < 0.05$. This difference in difficulty was attributed to two factors. First, the similarity of gender in the two items increases the difficulty. Second, it is harder to negate the meaning component male than the

meaning component female. When the first sentence is *A is the daughter of B*
no difference in difficulty was found between the item with *B is not the fa-*
ther of A and *B is not the mother of A* as the second sentence: Mann-Whitney-
U test $z = 1.44$, $p > 0.10$. The same result is found for the two items with
A is the mother of B as the first sentence: Mann-Whitney-U test $z = 0.42$,
$p > 0.60$. This result has been accounted for by the same two factors mentioned above: the similarity of the gender of the two terms and the male-female
asymmetry. These two factors are antagonistic in these items. No difference
in difficulty was found between *B is not the father of A* and *B is not the*
mother of A when the first sentence was *A is the child of B*: Mann-Whitney-U
test $z = 0.98$, $p > 0.30$. A rather speculative explanation has been given:
the male-female asymmetry in this case is counteracted by the fact that *child*
is more related to *mother* than to *father*.

These results lead to the following predictions for the present experiment.
If the first sentence contains the terms *son* or *father*, the RT for items with
a male term in the second sentence will be shorter than the RT for items with
a female term in the second sentence. When the first sentence contains the
term *daughter* or *mother*, the RT for items with a male term in the second sentence will be equal to the RT for items with a female term. The preference
for a male term is counteracted by the preference for a term of the same sex.
For items with *child* in the first sentence no difference is expected between
the *B is the father* and *B is the mother* item: the male-female asymmetry is
counteracted by the stronger association of *child* with *mother* than with *fa-*
ther.

11.1.1 Method

Material. Subjects were presented with two sentences. They had to judge
whether the second sentence could be true given the first sentence. Ten items
have been constructed which require the answer yes. The first sentence contained one of the kinship terms *father, mother, son, daughter*, and *child*,
e.g., *A is the son of B*. The second sentence contained a male or a female
kinship term of a different generation, e.g., *B is the mother of A*. Ten items
have been constructed which require the answer no. The kinship terms in these
items were, consequently, of the same generation. These items only served as
filler items in order to balance the yes and the no answers. The 20 experimental items were presented five times. The first presentation of the 20
items served as a practice block. The other four presentations constituted
the experimental blocks. Because the order of presentation was reversed for
two of these blocks and the first item to be presented was decided to be a

practice item, also the last item in a block had to be a practice item. Consequently, the 20 experimental items in a block were preceded and followed by one practice item.

The items were ordered in such a way that the first sentence in an item always differed from the first sentence in a consecutive item. The same is true for the second sentence in two consecutive items. No more than three consecutive items required the same answer.

Procedure. The items were presented by means of three slide projectors, one for the first sentence, one for the second sentence, and one for a blank interval between the items. The first sentence was presented for 2 s and was immediately followed by the second sentence. The time was measured from the onset of the second sentence until the subject pressed a button to indicate his answer. A blank interval of 4 s followed the answer. The equipment that has been described in Chapt. 3 was used for the presentation of the items and for the recording of the data.

Subjects. The subjects were ten male and ten female university students who volunteered in the experiment. They were paid for their participation. Five subjects from each sex group were run by a male experimenter and five by a female experimenter. The data of four more subjects have been eliminated from the analysis either because of high error rates or because of technical failures of the equipment.

11.1.2 Results

The average percentage of errors was 1.8%. No subject made more than 5% errors.

The results are presented in Table 11.1. Although the items requiring a no answer were only filler items, one remark should be made with respect to these items. The RT for these items was on the average 70 ms longer than for the items requiring a yes answer.

The data have been analyzed by means of an analysis of variance. The two between subjects factors were the sex of the experimenter and the sex of the subjects. The two within subjects factors were the kinship term in the first sentence with five levels and the gender of the kinship term in the second sentence.

The sex of the experimenter and the sex of the subjects had no effect on the RTs. The RT for the items differed depending on the kinship term of the first sentence: $F(4,144) = 4.51$, $p < 0.01$. This effect is mainly due to the difference between items that require an inference about parents and items that require an inference about children. The former type of item is easier

Table 11.1. Items, mean latencies [ms] in Experiment IV, and frequency of the answers in Experiment V

Item		Mean latency	Frequency	
A is the...of B;	B is the...of A[a]		first block[b]	all blocks[c]
son	father	1094	19	175
son	mother	1537	5	29
daughter	father	1396	10	67
daughter	mother	1277	16	138
child	father	1381	13	103
child	mother	1145	12	100
father	son	1521	22	157
father	daughter	1696	3	49
mother	son	1648	11	68
mother	daughter	1643	15	135
brother	brother	-	9	99
brother	sister	-	17	108
sister	brother	-	17	107
sister	sister	-	9	100

[a] Part of the stimulus in Experiment IV; part of the response in Experiment V.

[b] Maximum score = 26.

[c] Maximum score = 208.

than the latter: $F(1,144) = 17.59$, $p < 0.001$. This comparison accounts for 97% of the sum of squares between the items due to the first sentence. The second result was the interaction of the kinship term in the first sentence with the gender of the kinship term in the second sentence: $F(4,144) = 2.50$, $p < 0.05$. This interaction is not only due to the reversal of the male-female asymmetry for the items with child in the first sentence. The interaction of the gender in the first sentence with the gender in the second sentence, computed for the other four terms, is significant: $F(1,144) = 4.86$, $p < 0.05$.

If the first sentence contains a male kinship term, the RT for items with a male term in the second sentence is shorter than the RT for the items with a female term in the second sentence: $F(1,144) = 6.74$, $p < 0.05$. When the first sentence contains a female term, the RT for items with a male term in the second sentence is equal to the RT for items with a female term: $F(1,144) = 0.27$. These results confirm the predictions based on the two factors discussed above: the male-female asymmetry and the same-sex effect in the expectation of the subject. Contrary to the prediction, the items with *child* in the first sentence differed in RT; the RT for the item *B is the mother of A* is 236 ms shorter than for the item *B is the father of A*: $t(19) = 2.99$, $p < 0.01$.

11.1.3 Discussion

Items requiring an inference about parents were easier than items requiring an inference about children. This result may perhaps be accounted for by the place and the orientation of the subjects in their own families. These subjects were undergraduate students. They will consider themselves more easily as children than as parents. Their point of reference is son or daughter, not father or mother. In an experiment conducted by ROMNEY and D'ANDRADE (1964) subjects had to produce all the kinship terms that came to their minds. Almost all subjects reported the terms *father* and *mother*. However, less than one-third of the subjects reported the terms *son* and *daughter*. This orientation was also reflected in the order in which kinship terms were produced: parents were produced before children, if these were produced at all. These results have been replicated by NOORDMAN-VONK (1979) for Dutch subjects. Two other experiments of NOORDMAN-VONK (1979) illustrated the same orientation of the subjects. In one experiment subjects had to judge whether two kinship terms were of the same sex. In the other experiment they had to judge whether two kinship terms express a parent-child relation. In both experiments there appeared to be an order of searching information: parent terms are searched for earlier in the process than child terms.

Given the results of Experiment IV one discrepancy between Experiment I and Experiment III can be explained. Contrary to the expectations based on Experiment I, no difference was found between items with kinship terms of the same sex and items with kinship terms of different sex in condition I of Experiment III. This lack of difference was due mainly to the equal difficulty of the items with *not daughter* in the second sentence. The items with *not mother* in the second sentence in Experiment I, however, differed in RT. According to the results of the present experiment, the first sentence *A is the daughter of B* biases the expectation of the subject more to *B is the mother of A* than that *A is the mother of B* biases the expectation to *B is the daughter of A*. Similarly, *A is the son of B* biases the expectation more to *B is the mother of A* than that *A is the father of B* biases the expectation to *B is the daughter of A*. These two contrasts are part of the effect that inferences about parents are easier to make than inferences about children. The first discrepancy, however, is greater than the second one. Consequently, the extent to which the item *A is the daughter of B, B is not the mother of A* is more difficult than the item *A is the mother of B, B is not the daughter of A* should be greater than the extent to which the item *A is the son of B, B is not the mother of A* is more difficult than the item *A is the father of B, B is not the daughter of A*. Therefore, the difference in difficulty between the two items with *B is not the daughter of A* should be smaller than the difference in difficulty between the two items with *B is not the mother of A*, as was observed.

An assumption in the present experiment is that subjects process the information in the order in which it is presented: they make inferences with respect to the information in the second sentence on the basis of the information in the first sentence and not the other way around. Accordingly, it was assumed that the expectations with respect to *B* are created by the first sentence. This will be investigated further in the following experiment in which only one sentence is presented at a time.

11.2 Experiment V

In this experiment an item consisted of only one sentence, e.g., *A is the father of B*. Subjects had to tell what B most likely would be. The kinship terms *father, mother, son, daughter, child, brother,* and *sister* have been used. The predictions are the same as those in the previous experiment. They are based on the same two factors: the male-female asymmetry and the tendency to make an inference towards a kinship term of the same sex. For the items *A is the father of B* and *A is the son of B* it is expected that the frequency of the answers *son* and *father,* respectively, is greater than the frequency of the answers *daughter* and *mother,* respectively. Because of the antagonistic operations of the same two factors, no such difference is predicted for the items *A is the mother of B* and *A is the daughter of B*. Furthermore, no difference is expected for the item *A is the child of B*: the male-female asym-

136

metry and the relatively close relation of *child* with *mother* will counteract each other.

The predictions with respect to the terms *brother* and *sister* have yet to be specified. They are based on the basis of the result of Experiment III. No difference in difficulty was found between the items with *B is not the brother of A* and *B is not the sister of A* as the second sentence: Mann-Whitney-U test $z = 0.00$ for the items with *A is the brother of B* as the first sentence; $z = 0.34$ for the items with *A is the sister of B* as the first sentence. This lack of difference cannot be explained by the two antagonistic factors mentioned above, because these four items did not differ in difficulty at all. Brother and sister are symmetric terms. The gender is equally background in the two terms. Consequently, for the items *A is the brother of B* and *A is the sister of B* no difference in frequency is expected between the answers *B is the brother of A* and *B is the sister of A*.

11.2.1 Method

Material. The items have been presented in eight blocks of seven items each. Each block contained the seven kinship terms. The order of the items within the blocks and the order of the blocks were balanced.

Procedure. Items were presented again by means of a slide projector; a blank interval of 4 s followed the answer. The answers of the subjects were recorded on tape.

Subjects. The subjects were 13 male and 13 female university students, who volunteered in the experiment. They were paid for their participation.

11.2.2 Results

It was assumed that the answers for the first block would probably be more informative than the answer frequencies for all blocks together. Continuous presentation of the same items could easily induce a certain strategy in responding. Therefore, the analysis will primarily be based on the answers for the first block. The percentage of errors for the whole experiment was on the average 1.5%. Only one subject made more than two errors; this subject responded six times with *child* or *parent*. The results are presented in Table 11.1.

No differences were found between male and female subjects. The frequencies of the answers for male and female subjects were almost equal for each item.

The predictions are confirmed by the data. For the items *A is the father of B* and *A is the son of B* the male term was given as the answer more frequently than the female term: $\chi^2(1) = 14.44$, $p < 0.001$; $\chi^2(1) = 8.17$, $p < 0.01$, respectively. No difference is found for the items *A is the mother of B* and *A is the daughter of B*: $\chi^2(1) = 0.62$, $p > 0.30$; $\chi^2(1) = 1.38$, $p > 0.20$, respectively. Accordingly, the answers are again determined by the same two factors: the male-female asymmetry and the preference to make an inference towards a term of the same sex as the presented term. These effects can be tested for the four items together. Averaging the frequencies for these four items, the mean frequency for a male term is 5.75 greater than the mean frequency for a female term: Wilcoxon matched-pairs signed-ranks $z = 2.26$, $p < 0.025$. The mean frequency for a term of the same sex as the presented term is 11.75 greater than the mean frequency of a term of the opposite sex: $z = 3.30$, $p < 0.01$.

Treating the frequencies of the answers over all blocks leads to essentially the same conclusion. First, there is a tendency to respond with a term of the same sex. Second, the tendency to respond with a male term is stronger than to respond with a female term. The only difference is that the same-sex effect is significant also for the items *A is the daughter of B* and *A is the mother of B*: sign test $\chi^2(1) = 9.00$, $p < 0.01$; $\chi^2(1) = 7.35$, $p < 0.01$, respectively. Apparently, the tendency to respond with a term of the same sex becomes more pronounced with repeated presentation of the same items.

The predictions with respect to the *brother, sister,* and *child* items are also confirmed by the data. The difference between a male and a female answer for *A is the brother of B* in the first block is not significant: $\chi^2(1) = 2.46$, $p > 0.10$. The same result is found for the item *A is the sister of B*. Again the analysis of all blocks leads to the same conclusion.

11.2.3 Discussion

The results of Experiments IV and V are in agreement with those of the previous experiments. These experiments demonstrated that people more easily assume that a person is male than that a person is female. In the previous experiments it was found that the meaning component male is harder to negate than the meaning component female. Both the present experiments and the previous experiments illustrate the difference in presupposed or background information of the meaning components male and female. The second result of the present experiments is that the information given in the first sentence determines the expectation about the new information: subjects are inclined to assume that person B is of the same sex as person A. This result is in agreement with the fact that a negation of a kinship term of the same sex increases the difficulty of the problems in the previous experiments.

The same two factors appeared in an experiment performed by NOORDMAN-VONK (1979). When subjects have to judge whether two terms express a parent-child relation, the RT is shorter when the terms are of the same sex than when they are not. Moreover, the RT for items *father son* and *mother son* was shorter than for the items *father daughter* and *mother daughter*, respectively. This illsutrates again the male-female asymmetry.

In one respect the results of the present experiment differ from those of the previous experiments. The male-female asymmetry and the facilitating effect of kinship terms of the same sex in both sentences cancel each other out when the first sentence contains a female kinship term. Without testing, the relative importance of these two factors can be described by comparing the mean differences in RT due to these factors. The similarity of gender accounts for a greater proportion of the variance between the items than the male-female asymmetry: the mean difference between the items with kinship terms of the same sex and kinship terms of opposite sex is 186 ms; the mean difference between the items with a male and with a female term in the second sentence is 124 ms. The opposite is found in the previous negation experiments. The difference between the items due to the male-female asymmetry was greater than the difference due to similarity or dissimilarity in sex of the two kinship terms. The conclusion is that the difficulty of the items in the previous negation experiments is not exclusively determined by the expectations induced by the first sentence. The second sentence is important in determining the difficulty of the problems: it is more difficult to negate the male than to negate the female meaning component.

On the basis of the results of the present experiment, one can quantify the strength of the expectations and relate these expectations to the results of the Experiments I and III. Actually, the present experiment indicates for the items with *father, mother, son,* and *daughter* first, that subjects assume in 61% of the cases that B is male and in 39% of the cases that B is female (male-female asymmetry) and second, that subjects assume in 71% of the cases that B is of the same sex as A and in 29% of the cases that B is of the opposite sex (same-sex effect). Thus, the strength of the expectation that B is male can be expressed in terms of probability: $p = 0.61$. The strength of the expectation that B is of the same sex is expressed by the probability $p = 0.71$. On the basis of these two effects, the inferential processes for the items in Experiments I and III can be formalized in the following way. Based on the first sentence, a subject infers with a probability of 0.61 that B is male (male-female asymmetry) and with a probability of 0.71 that B is of the same sex as A (same-sex effect). It has been demonstrated that the male-female effect is also due to the second sentence: the negation in the second sentence is less likely to affect the male than the female component; one assumes with a probability of 0.61 that B is male. These parameters are considered as indices of strength for a particular answer. The strength of the expectation for the incorrect answer has been expressed by averaging the relevant parameters for each item. These scores as well as the proportion of incorrect answers per item are presented in Table 11.2. The Spearman rank correlation between strength of expectation for incorrect answers and proportion of incorrect answers is $\varrho = 0.93$.

Table 11.2. Proportion of incorrect answers (Experiments I and III) and strength of expectations for incorrect answers as predicted from Experiment V

Item A is the...of B;	B is not the...of A	Strength of expectation for incorrect answer	Proportion of incorrect answer
son	father	0.64	0.88
son	mother	0.36	0.00
daughter	father	0.50	0.47
daughter	mother	0.50	0.29
father	son	0.64	0.70
father	daughter	0.36	0.10
mother	son	0.50	0.30
mother	daughter	0.50	0.30

Two remarks should be made with respect to this analysis. First, the strength of the expectation for the incorrect answer is only a relative index. These strengths express the difficulty of the items as compared to each other. They do not express the probability of an incorrect answer. Actually, subjects may be able to get rid of these expectations by analyzing only the information that is presented. Second, background information is defined in this chapter with respect to expectations. Accordingly, the strength of the expectations is a quantification of the background character of the information. The procedure outlined above consists of quantifying the background character of the information and illustrates to what extent the background information is brought about by the first sentence and by the second sentence.

Chapter 12   Variability of Foreground and Background Information

Many word pairs in natural language have an asymmetry like the one that was
found for the word pairs *father mother* and *son daughter*. Examples are marked-unmarked word pairs such as *good* and *bad*, *long* and *short*, and positive
and negative prepositions like *above* and *below*. Similar psychological phenomena have been found for these categories of concepts as well as for the
kinship terms *father* and *mother*. In a task in which subjects had to recall
comparative sentences (CLARK and CARD, 1969) adjectives tended to change
from marked to unmarked form over time more than from unmarked to marked:
bad is recalled as *good* more frequently than *good* is recalled as *bad*. In a
task where subjects were required to change *isn't above* into *below* and to
change *isn't below* into *above*, the transformation towards the unmarked form
took less time than the transformation towards the marked form (YOUNG and
CHASE, 1971). In word association tasks there appears to be a tendency to
change a feature from its marked form rather than to its marked form (CLARK,
1970b; MARSHALL, 1969). With respect to marked and unmarked words, e.g.,
good and *bad*, CLARK (1969a, 1969b, 1974) distinguishes between the nominal
sense of *good* as in *how good was the film* and the contrastive sense of *good*
as in *the film was good*. A marked word has only the contrastive sense. These
senses are represented by CLARK in the following feature notation: *good* in
the nominal sense has the components [+ evaluative (polar)]; in the contrastive sense it had the components [+ evaluative (+ polar)], *bad* has the components [+ evaluative (- polar)]. The asymmetry consists of the fact that the
nominal sense which exists only for the unmarked concept is simpler because
it is not specified for polarity. For the positive and negative prepositions
CLARK proposes the following feature notation: *above* is coded as [+ vertical
(+ polar)]; *below* as [+ vertical (- polar)]. The asymmetry is now explained
by postulating that the coding + is more easily abtained than the coding -.
This explanation is also offered as an alternative explanation of the asymmetry between marked and unmarked words. According to FODOR (1975, p.147),
however, these representations, which define the complexity of the words,

do not account for the asymmetry between *John is tall* and *John is short* as observed in psychological processes.

An intriguing question is where this asymmetry comes from. Why is masculinity more background information than femininity in the previous experiments; why can only *good* be used in a nominal sense and not *bad*. There are certainly biological, educational, and cultural factors involved. CLARK (1973a) discussed spatial words in this respect. This problem, however, will not be discussed at present. The question to be studied now is how the asymmetry should be described. Is it due to the lexical coding of the concepts themselves or is it due to the use of the concepts? In other words, can the asymmetry be sufficiently described in terms of differential lexical coding of the concepts or does the asymmetry depend on factors such as foreground and background? The problem to be studied at present is whether the asymmetry between male and female kinship terms can be influenced by manipulating the foreground and background information.

In terms of background and foreground information, the asymmetry consists of the fact that a particular meaning component, e.g., gender, is more background information in one word than in another word. In that case, the asymmetry should disappear if that component is stressed as the focus of communication. In terms of lexical coding, however, the asymmetry consists of the fact that the positive value of the meaning component can more easily be represented than the negative value. This asymmetry will not disappear if that meaning component is stressed. Experiments with marked and unmarked words provide evidence for the foreground-background theory (Part I).

The following experiment together with Experiment IV deals with this problem for kinship terms. The task in Experiment IV was such that the attention of the subject was directed to the generation. The task in fact stressed the generation component as the criterion against which the subject had to make his decision. The answer is yes if and only if the kinship term in the second sentence is of another generation than the kinship term in the first sentence. It is clear that the gender component is quite irrelevant for the decision: if *A is the father of B*, *B* can be the son, but also the daughter of *A*. The vast majority of the subjects spontaneously reported that they had used the generation as the criterion for their answers.

The results gave evidence for the male-female asymmetry as was expected on the basis of both the foreground-background theory and the theory of lexical coding. In the following experiment the attention of the subject was directed to the sex of the kinship terms.

142

12.1 Experiment VI

Subjects were told they had to make a judgment with respect to the sex of
kinship terms. An item consisted of two sentences in the following form: *A
is the father of B, A is male.* The subjects had to decide whether the second
sentence was true or not, given the first sentence. Items have been constructed with the terms *father, mother, son, daughter, brother,* and *sister* for the
first sentence and with the concepts *male* and *female* for the second sentence.
According to the theory of lexical coding, the latency for the male items
should be shorter than for the female items for the same reason as in Experiment IV. According to the theory of foreground-background information, the
latencies should not differ, because the gender is in both cases equally in
the foreground.

12.1.1 Method

Material. The items are presented in Table 12.1. The twelve experimental
items were presented seven times in different order. The experimental items

Table 12.1. Items and mean latencies [ms] in Experiment VI

| Item | | Sex of subjects | |
A is the ... of B;	A is ...	male	female
father	male	587	683
father	female	662	742
mother	male	699	665
mother	female	609	607
son	male	539	659
son	female	597	723
daughter	male	657	654
daughter	female	631	608
brother	male	591	695
brother	female	637	759
sister	male	641	642
sister	female	617	623

were preceded and followed by some practice items. Moreover, the first block
was a practice block.

   Procedure. The procedure was the same as in Experiment IV: the items were
presented by means of slide projectors. Again, the two sentences of an item
were presented one after the other, and the time was measured from the onset
of the presentation of the second sentence until the subject gave his answer.

   Subjects. Twenty-four university students volunteered in the experiment;
they were paid for their participation. The experiment was balanced with respect to the sex of the experimenter and with respect to the sex of the subjects.

12.1.2 Results

The results are presented in Table 12.1. There was a significant yes-no effect. The RT for items requiring a yes answer was 52 ms shorter than the RT
for items requiring a no answer: $F(1,20) = 16.82$; $p < 0.001$. Because the
items requiring a yes answer are of primary interest and because the results
for the yes items yield the same pattern as the results for the no items,
only the former results will be discussed.

   The RT for the male terms was not different from the RT for the female
terms: $F(1,20) = 0.31$. The RT for, e.g., *A is the father of B, A is male*
was not different from the RT for *A is the mother of B, A is female* as was
predicted by the foreground-background theory.

   However, an interaction effect was found between the sex of the subjects
and the sex of the kinship terms. The RT was shorter when the sex of the
subject and the sex of the terms were the same than when they were different: $F(1,20) = 9.74$; $p < 0.01$. This difference was 47 and 66 ms for male
and female subjects, respectively. This effect cannot be explained by a general preference of male subjects for the answer *male* and of female subjects
for the answer *female*, independently of the information of the first sentence.
In fact, considering all the items in the experiment, male subjects responded
to *male* only 7 ms quicker than to *female* and female subjects did the same,
the difference being 11 ms. Moreover, the interaction of the sex of subjects
with the gender of the kinship term in the first sentence was significant:
$F(1,40) = 14.00$; $p < 0.001$. Consequently, the first sentence has an influence
on the expectations.

12.1.3 Discussion

The present results cannot be accounted for by the theory of lexical coding.
Ease of processing the concepts cannot satisfactorily be described in terms

of the lexical coding of the concepts. First, male terms are not always easier to process than female terms. Second, the theory of lexical coding cannot explain that female terms are easier to process by female subjects when the sex is stressed, but not when the sex is not stressed.

On the other hand, the theory of foreground-background information has to be qualified. The foreground-background distinction does not depend only on the verbal context, but also on the personal context of the subject. In some cases there may be an interaction of the material with the situation of the subject. This may be called the orientation of the subject, or his ego involvement. An example of this interaction has been discussed in Experiment IV: inferences about parents were easier to make than inferences about children. The asymmetry between male and female kinship terms can be described in terms of foreground and background as follows. If the gender is not stressed, male is more background information than female. It is more difficult to negate the meaning component male than the component female; it is easier to take the meaning component male for granted. If, however, the gender is stressed, the meaning components male and female become foreground information. Due to the personal involvement of the subject with the material, or more precisely with the decisive feature gender in this case, male is more foreground than female for male subjects and female is more foreground than male for female subjects. By the way, the male-female asymmetry is now symmetric (!).

This personal orientation of the subject is also found in an experiment performed by NOORDMAN-VONK (1979). When subjects have to judge whether two concepts are of the same sex, male subjects start processing male terms and female subjects start processing female terms.

The situation in Experiment IV was analogous. The decisive feature was generation. Accordingly, the subjects reacted as children of their generation.

Another confirmation of the present theory comes from material that has no relation with the personal situation of the subject. It is generally found that unmarked words, e.g., *big, high*, are easier to process than marked words, e.g., *small, low*. If, however, the feature on which the words differ is stressed, the asymmetry disappears, as predicted by the present theory. If a subject knows that he has to answer a question, e.g., *which one is the highest* or *which one is the lowest*, and if the required information is not stored in a way congruent with one of these questions, there is no difference in RT between the marked and the unmarked question (Part I).

The conclusion is that the asymmetry between male and female kinship terms as well as between unmarked and marked adjectives depends on the background-foreground distinction. The asymmetry cannot sufficiently be described in terms of lexical coding. Marked and unmarked words are asymmetric when the feature on which they differ is in the background. When this feature is in the foreground, marked and unmarked words are symmetric in the psychological processes.

Conclusion

The results of the present experiments lead to the conclusion that the meaning components of the kinship terms differ with respect to foreground and background information. Foreground information is explicitly communicated information; background information is not the proper content of the message; it is assumed to be true. In general the generation is the foreground information of the problems being studied, and gender is the background information. For whatever reason, however, the masculinity of many male kinship terms is more background information than the femininity of the corresponding female terms. When processing a negation, one searches for the meaning component the negation refers to, starting with the information that is most in the foreground. This explains the difficulty of the riddles in the three negation experiments as well as the asymmetry between the riddles with male and female kinship terms. That masculinity is more background information and more likely presupposed than femininity accounts also for the results of the three latter experiments in which a decision had to be made with respect to gender or generation. Explaining the asymmetry between male and female kinship terms as well as between unmarked and marked adjectives in terms of background and foreground information has the advantage that one can easil account for the effects of contextual factors, linguistic or psychological, on reasoning tasks with these terms.

Chapter 13   Summary and Conclusions

13.1 Summary

Comprehension in the present study is characterized as a process of integrating new information with old information. This process is considered to include inferential processes, as is discussed in the first chapter. The new
information in this study is presented in the form of sentences. The study
consists of three parts that differ with respect to what information is treated as old information. In the first part comprehension deals with the integration of information in sentences with information in other sentences. The
materials that are studied are comparative constructions. The emphasis in
the second part is on the integration of information in sentences with knowledge of the world. The verbal material consists of conditional sentences.
The third part deals again with the comprehension of sentences with respect
to knowledge of the world. In this part, the notion of old information is
extended so as to include pragmatic factors such as certain presuppositions
and expectations. The verbal material consists of kinship terms.

   Comprehension is studied from an information processing point of view.
The dependent variable in most of the experiments is the reaction time (RT).

13.1.1 Part I: Comparative Relations

The main question in this part is how reasoning processes are to be characterized and how the processes depend on the way the information is coded.
This is studied by varying the complexity of the information and by varying
the time that is allowed for the coding process. The experimental material
consists of three-term series problems. The items vary in complexity: the
more complex items are negative equatives such as *Marc is not as small as
Paul, Paul is not as small as Dave, who is biggest?*; the less complex items
are comparatives such as *Paul is smaller than Marc, Paul is bigger than Dave,
who is biggest?*. The results of the first experiment in which the question
is presented simultaneously with the propositions give evidence for the following conclusions. The processing of the less complex items is characterized

in terms of the semantic distinction between marked and unmarked adjectives.
The processing of the more complex items, on the other hand, is much more
characterized by the syntactic surface characteristics of the sentences. The
more complex items are analyzed in relation to the question, which reduces
the complexity of the task. The information processed most recently is most
available. A model is constructed that accounts for the data. On the basis
of this model predictions are made for the subsequent experiments.

In the second, third, and fourth experiments the question is separated
from the propositions by delay increasing in length from 0 to 4 and 8 s,
respectively. Two latencies are measured for each item: the inspection time
and the answering time. The inspection times are predictable on the basis of
the model. The results of the answering times indicate that the longer the
time available for the coding, the more the information tends to be coded
in the basic representation of the positive, unmarked form. This code was
reached for the comparative items earlier than for the negative equative
items. When the time interval was 8 s, both positive and negative information was coded in the basic unmarked form. After such an interval effects due
to the surface structure of the sentences are no longer observed. The answering process for each experiment is characterized in terms of the congruence or incongruence of the question with the form in which the information is coded after the time interval.

In order to investigate whether the observed inference processes generalize to other material as well, a similar task was devised with nonverbal,
pictorial information. The results of Experiments V and VI show that basical-
ly the same processes are involved as in the verbal tasks: the information
processed most recently is most available; analyzing the information in relation to the question may reduce the complexity of the task. As was expected, no marked-unmarked effect of the question was found, which indicates that
the information is coded in a different way than in the previous experiments.
This confirms that the marked-unmarked effect found in the previous experiments is due to the congruence between the coding of the stored information
and the coding of the question. The absence of the marked-unmarked effect
suggests that such an effect depends on the foreground character of the feature on which the words differ.

13.1.2 Part II. Conditional Relations

This part deals with the comprehension of sentences with respect to knowledge
of the world. The first chapter of this part concerns the question to what
extent the interpretation of conditional sentences depends on the meaning one

attributes to the conditional conjunction and to what extent it depends on the knowledge of the world expressed in the sentence. As far as this latter aspect is concerned, three types of sentences are studied: sentences with a biconditional context, such as *if it is freezing, the temperature is below $32^{O}F$*; sentences with a conditional context, such as *if it is raining, the streets are wet*; and sentences with an arbitrary context, such as *if the red light is lit, the blue one is lit*. Sentences are constructed with the conjunctions *if ... then, either ... or, unless,* and *only if*. A reasoning experiment indicates that all the conditional conjunctions are interpreted predominantly as biconditionals in all the kinds of contexts, although this is true to a smaller extent for *if ... then* than for the other conjunctions. Thus, the conjunctions establish a bidirectional link between the propositions in the clauses as well as between the negated propositions. This biconditionality is described in terms of old and new information. Each proposition and its negation can function as a direct antecedent to which a subsequent sentence can refer.

The biconditional interpretation of conditional sentences is accounted for by pragmatic factors in communication, in particular by the knowledge that is presupposed by the speaker and listener and which functions as background information. The number of errors in this experiment indicates that the conjunctions *unless* and *either ... or* are the most difficult to handle.

In the second experiment six sentences dealing with the same event are judged as same or different in meaning. The results indicate a difference in the pragmatic function of a conditional sentence viz. between condition-consequence relations, e.g., *if John is ill, he is not going to his work* and inference relations, e.g., *if John is not going to his work, he is ill*.

The third experiment concerns the question as to how a conditional relatio is stored and reproduced. The conjunction *if ... then* appears to be the most basic conjunction of those being studied, in the sense that conditional sentences tend to be reproduced as *if ... then* sentences. Moreover, it appears that the distinction between condition-consequence relations and inference relations is an important factor in the memory processes.

In the final experiment subjects have to verify conditional sentences. The RT for the judgments was measured. The factors found in the previous experiments could account for the RTs in the present experiment. The part on conditional relations closes with a model for the comprehension of conditional sentences. Comprehension in this model is described in terms of the following operations: the sentence is transformed into a cognitive representation; factual knowledge is retrieved in a representation as congruent as possible with the sentence representation; these representations are matched with each other.

13.1.3 Part III. Foreground and Background Information

This part is concerned again with the comprehension of sentences with respect to knowledge of the world but now conceived in a pragmatic way. The knowledge of the world that is studied consists of information that is presupposed and assumed by the speaker and listener. This information is called background information as opposed to foreground information which is explicitly communicated in the sentence. This foreground-background distinction is studied in inference tasks with kinship terms. It was assumed that the gender is the background information for these terms. This is confirmed by the first experiment in which riddles were given consisting of a positive sentence containing a child term and a negative sentence containing a parent term, e.g., *A is the son of B; B is not the father of A. How is that possible?*. The negation in the second sentence of the riddle is hardly or never interpreted by subjects as applying to the gender of the kinship terms. But if the gender is affected by the negation, it is more frequently the gender female than male. Thus, there appears to be a male-female asymmetry: the feature male is more difficult to negate than the feature female. The difficulty of the negation is also affected by the context: if kinship terms of both genders are mentioned in the riddle, the gender is more easily affected by the negation; this is called the same-sex effect. In the second experiment the hypotheses are tested that a negation tends to affect only one meaning component (principle of minimal negation) and that this component is parenthood. These hypotheses are confirmed. Based on linguistic evidence it is expected that the asymmetry for kinship terms *father* and *mother* will be replicated by the terms *son* and *daughter* but not by *brother* and *sister*. This is found, indeed, in Experiment III. In all cases the gender appeared to be the background information.

    In the following experiments the dependency of the foreground-background distinction on verbal and nonverbal context is illustrated. Experiments IV and V investigate the role of the affirmative, i.e., the first sentence of the riddles in creating the background information. The factors which played a role in the previous experiments, the male-female asymmetry and the same-sex effect, are operative again. The results of Experiment V gave the possibility to compute the strength of the background information for the riddles of Experiments I and III. These strength scores correlate highly with the difficulty of solving these riddles. Furthermore, the personal orientation of the subject appears to be important: inferences about parents are more easily made than inferences about children. Experiment VI demonstrates the dependency of the foreground-background distinction on the task. The task stresses the gender of the terms. Consequently, the gender should be foreground information, and the male-female asymmetry should disappear. This is, indeed, found. The results suggest that subjects process kinship terms of their own sex earlier than kinship terms of the opposite sex. Thus, the personal orientation of the subject affects the foreground information.

Background information appears to be very similar to the given information as studied by CLARK and HAVILAND. It can be considered as a pragmatic extension of this notion. It differs from given information in the sense that background information is not identified as given in the sentence but is presupposed to be given. Secondly, background information as defined with respect to the expectations can vary in strength.

13.2 Conclusions

The results of the present study lead to the following conclusions with respect to verbal information processing. The processing of information can be described as a process of complexity reduction. Comprehension processes depend on the congruence of the pieces of information that have to be integrated: comprehension is achieved by making the coding of the pieces of information congruent to one another. The processing of linguistic information cannot sufficiently be accounted for in terms of linguistic variables, but instead is relative to pragmatic factors. These conclusions will be illustrated in some detail.

Man as complexity reducer. The results of the experiments on comparatives indicate a gradual transformation of the coded information into a basic form: negative information is coded positively (the information was dichotomous); the information is ultimately coded in unmarked form. When subjects have to process complex information, they make use of strategies that reduce the complexity of the processing as indicated by the analysis of verbal and pictorial information in relation to the question.

Similar conclusions emerge from the experiments on conditional relations. *Unless* sentences are reproduced as *if ... then* sentences (Experiment II); the errors in the reasoning task of Experiment I and the RTs in Experiment IV indicated that *unless* is more complex than *if ... then* and even more complex than *if ... then* with an added negation. Again, negative information is coded positively if the information is dichotomous: the two negatives in *unless not* cancel each other. Furthermore, the basic form of the coding of conditional sentences is the condition-consequence form. The coding of the more complex inference relations makes use of this basic form. Finally, if the information is very complex and confusing, the complexity is reduced by escaping form the task.

The principle of minimal negation, found in the third part, is an economic strategy to handle a negation: only the meaning component that is most in the foreground is negated.

Comprehension and congruence. The general and fundamental property of the comprehension processes, as described in all three parts, is that the nature of comprehension processes is determined by the extent to which the pieces of information are congruent to one another. In each experiment on the comparatives, the answering process is determined by the congruence or incongruence between the question and the form of the stored information. If the information is not congruent, an extra operation is required to make it congruent. Similarly, an important principle of the model for conditional sentences is that the representation of the conditional relation retrieved from stored knowledge is as congruent as possible with the representation of the sentence. This principle is true for the coding of the clauses. It is also illustrated by the difficulty of understanding an inference relation. This difficulty is described in terms of an incongruence between sentence code and stored knowledge.

Two more observations, both described in terms of given and new information, illustrate the importance of congruent coding in the comprehension process. The absence of a direct antecedent for given information can be considered as an incongruence between given information and available information. This incongruence can be handled by an extra operation, e.g., bridging or reconstitution. The first observation concerns the comparatives. The RT is longer when, after the negative transformation, the new term is not the subject in the sentence than when it is the subject. The incongruence between what is actually new and old information and what is new and old information according to the structure of the sentence is handled by a reconstitution by which the new term is made the subject of the sentence. The second observation concerns the interpretation of conditional sentences. It is argued that *only if* establishes a bidirectional relation both between the clauses expressed in the sentence and between their negations. The latter is not always true for *if ... then* sentences. In such a case, the negated clause in the *if ... then* sentences are not given information, and an inference from such a negated clause will less likely be made, because it requires a bridging operation. The incongruence results in the positive equivalence interpretation of *if* ... *then*.

The importance of the congruence of the information is also illustrated by the experiments on kinship terms. An incongruence between presupposed information and intended information, as is observed in the negation experiments, greatly impairs the comprehension process; an inference can hardly or not at all be made.

Linguistic versus pragmatic factors. The processes in the comprehension of linguistic information are determined not only by the linguistic variables of the input but also, and to a large extent, by pragmatic factors such as certain presuppositions and expectations that constitute the background information. Thus, an essentialistic account of verbal processing in terms of linguistic structures will not be adequate. This is expecially clear from the results in Part III. The main results of these experiments are desribed in terms of foreground and background information: the difficulty of negating the gender, the greater difficulty of negating the male than the female component, and the stronger tendency to infer a male term rather than a female term. It is demonstrated that the effects due to the foreground-background distinction can indeed be influenced by manipulating the foreground and background information. This has been achieved by stressing certain information in the task. Another nonlinguistic variable which plays a role in determining what information is foreground and what is background and which, accordingly, influences the inference processes is the personal orientation of the subject.

The role of foreground and background is also found in the experiments on comparatives and on conditionals. The difference in difficulty between the processing of marked and unmarked adjectives disappears when the polarity of the adjectives is stressed by the task. Similarly, there is no difference in difficulty between the retrieval of positive and negative information when the positive and negative character of the information is focussed upon in the task. Finally, the fact that conditional sentences are interpreted as biconditional sentences is accounted for in terms of background information. The meaning of a conditional sentence and of verbal information in general is not exclusively determined by the sentence, but all kinds of pragmatic factors play a role. Inferring from language requires inferring beyond language.

References

Ach, N. (1905): *Ueber die Willenstätigkeit und das Denken* (Vandenhoeck & Ruprecht, Göttingen)

Anderson, J.R. (1974): Verbatim and propositional representation of sentences in immediate and long-term memory. J. Verbal Learning Verbal Behav. *13*, 149-162

Anderson, J.R., Bower, G.H. (1973): *Human Associative Memory* (Winston, Washington, D.C.)

Austin, J.L. (1963): "Performative-Constative", in *Philosophy and Ordinary Language*, ed. by C.E. Caton (University of Illinois Press, Urbana)

Benjafield, J., Doan, B. (1971): Similarities between memory for visually perceived relations and comparative sentences. Psychon. Sc. *24*, 255-256

Blumenthal, A.L. (1974): "An Historical View of Psycholinguistics", in *Current Trends in Linguistics*, Vol. XII, ed. by T.A. Sebeok (Mouton, The Hague)

Bobrow, D.G., Collins, A. (Eds.) (1975): *Representation and Understanding* (Academic Press, New York)

Bower, G.H. (1972): "Mental Imagery and Associative Learning", in *Cognition in Learning and Memory*, ed. by L.W. Gregg (Wiley, New York)

Bransford, J.D., Barclay, J.R., Franks, J.J. (1972): Sentence memory: A constructive versus interpretive approach. Cognitive Psychol. *3*, 193-209

Bransford, J.D., Franks, J.J. (1972): The abstraction of linguistic ideas: A review. Cognition *1*, 211-250

Bransford, J.D., Johnson, M.K. (1973): " Considerations of Some Problems of Comprehension", in *Visual Information Processing*, ed. by W.G. Chase (Academic Press, New York)

Brée, D.S. (1973): "The Interpretation of Implication", in *Artificial and Human Thinking*, ed. by A. Elithorn, D. Jones (Elsevier, Amsterdam)

Brée, D.S., Coppens, G. (1972): "The Interpretation Given to a Conditional Sentence Affects the Way It Is Validated". Interfaculty for Graduate Studies in Management (Rotterdam)

Brée, D.S., Meerum-Terwogt, M. (1971): "The Relationship Between Performance on Different Tasks". Interfaculty for Graduate Studies in Management (Rotterdam)

Breuker, J.A. (1976): Semantic Memory. Nederlands Tijdschrift voor de Psychologie *31*, 131-151

Bruner, J.S., Goodnow, J.J., Austin, G.A. (1956): *A Study of Thinking* (Wiley, New York)

Carpenter, P.A. (1973): Extracting information from counterfactual clauses. J. Verbal Learning Verbal Behav. *12*, 512-521

Carpenter, P.A. (1974): On the comprehension, storage, and retrieval of comparative sentences. J. Verbal Learning Verbal Behav. *13*, 401-411

Carpenter, P.A., Just, M.A. (1975): Sentence comprehension: A psycholinguistic processing model of verification. Psychol. Rev. *82*, 45-73

Carpenter, P.A., Just, M.A. (1976): Models of sentence verification and linguistic comprehension. Psychol. Rev. *83*, 318-322

156

Carroll, J.B. (1972): "Defining Language Comprehension: Some Speculations",
 in *Language Comprehension and the Acquisition of Knowledge*, ed. by
 R.O. Freedle, J.B. Carroll (Winston, Washington, D.C.)
Chafe, W.L. (1970): *Meaning and the Structure of Language* (University of
 Chicago Press, Chicago)
Chafe, W.L. (1972): "Discourse Structure and Human Knowledge", in *Language
 Comprehension and Acquisition of Knowledge*, ed. by R.O. Freedle,
 J.B. Carroll (Winston, Washington, D.C.)
Chase, W.G. Clark, H.H. (1972): "Mental Operations in the Comparison of
 Sentences and Pictures, in *Cognition in Learning and Memory*, ed. by
 L.W. Gregg (Wiley, New York)
Chomsky, N. (1968): *Language and Mind* (Harcourt Brace Jovanovich, New York)
Chomsky, N. (1971): "Deep Structure, Surface Structure and Semantic Inter-
 pretation", in *Semantics: An Interdisciplinary Reader in Philosophy,
 Linguistics and Psychology*, ed. by L.A. Jakobovits, D.D. Steinberg
 (Cambridge University Press, Cambridge)
Clark, H.H. (1969a): Linguistic processes in deductive reasoning. Psychol.
 Rev. *76*, 387-404
Clark, H.H. (1969b): The influence of language in solving three-term series
 problems. J. Exp. Psychol. *82*, 205-215
Clark, H.H. (1970a): "Comprehending Comparatives", in *Advances in Psycho-
 linguistics*, ed. by G.B. Flores d' Arcais, W.J.M. Levelt (North-Holland
 Publishing Co., Amsterdam)
Clark, H.H. (1970b): "Word Associations and Linguistic Theory", in *New
 Horizons in Linguistics*, ed. by J. Lyons (Penguin Books, Harmondsworth)
Clark, H.H. (1971): More about "adjectives, comparatives, and syllogisms":
 A reply to Huttenlocher and Higgins. Psychol. Rev. *78*, 505-514
Clark, H.H. (1972a): Difficulties people have in answering the question
 "where is it?". J. Verbal Learning Verbal Behav. *11*, 265-277
Clark, H.H. (1972b): On the evidence concerning J. Huttenlocher and E.T.
 Higgins' theory of reasoning: A second reply. Psychol. Rev. *79*, 428-431
Clark, H.H. (1973a): "Space, Time, Semantics, and the Child", in *Cognitive
 Development and the Acquisition of Language*, ed. by T.E. Moore (Academic
 Press, New York)
Clark, H.H. (1973b): "Comprehension and the Given-New Contract". Paper pre-
 sented at the Conference on the Role of Grammar in Interdisciplinary
 Linguistic Research, University of Bielefeld, Bielefeld, Germany
Clark, H.H. (1973c): The language-as-fixed-effect fallacy: A critique of
 language statistics in psychological research. J. Verbal Learning Verbal
 Behav. *12*, 335-359
Clark, H.H. (1974): "Semantics and Comprehension", in *Current Trends in
 Linguistics*, Vol. XII, ed. by T.A. Sebeok (Mouton, The Hague)
Clark, H.H. (1978): "Inferring What Is Meant", in *Studies in the Perception
 of Language*, ed. by W.J.M. Levelt, G.B. Flores d'Arcais (Wiley, New York)
 New York)
Clark, H.H., Card, S.K. (1969): Role of semantics in remembering comparative
 sentences. J. Exp. Psychol. *82*, 545-553
Clark, H.H., Carpenter, P.A., Just, M.A. (1973): "On the Meeting of Semantics
 and Perception", in *Visual Information Processing*, ed. by W.G. Chase
 (Academic Press, New York)
Clark, H.H., Chase, W.G. (1972): On the Process of comparing sentences against
 pictures. Cognitive Psychol. *3*, 472-517
Clark, H.H., Cohen, J., Keith Smith, J.E., Keppel, G. (1976): Discussion of
 Wike and Church's comments. J. Verbal Learning Verbal Behav. *15*, 257-266
Clark, H.H., Haviland, S.E. (1974): "Psychological Processes as Linguistic
 Explanation", in *Explaining Linguistic Phenomena*, ed. by D. Cohen
 (Hemisphere Publishing Co., Washington, D.C.)

Clark, H.H., Haviland, S.E. (1977): "Comprehension and the Given-New Contract", in *Discourse Production and Comprehension*, ed. by R.O. Freedle (Ablex Publishing, Norwood, N.J.)

Clark, H.H., Lucy, P. (1975): Understanding what is meant from what is said: A study in conversationally conveyed requests. J. Verbal Learning Verbal Behav. *14*, 56-72

Collins, A.M., Loftus, E.F. (1975): A spreading-activation theory of semantic processing. Psychol. Rev. *82*, 407-428

Craik, F.I.M., Lockhart, R.S. (1972): Levels of processing: A framework for memory research. J. Verbal Learning Verbal Behav. *11*, 671-684

De Groot, A.D. (1965): *Thought and Choice in Chess* (Mouton, The Hague)

De Soto, C., London, M., Handel, S. (1965): Social reasoning and spatial paralogic. J. Personality Soc. Psychol. *2*, 513-521

Donders, F.C. (1868): Over de snelheid van psychische processen. Onderzoekingen gedaan in het Physiologisch Laboratorium der Utrechtsche Hoogeschool, 1868-1869, *2*, 92-120. [Transl. by W.G. Koster in *Attention and Performance II*, ed. by W.G. Koster, 1969, Acta Psychol. *30*, 412-431]

Fillenbaum, S. (1973): *Syntactic Factors in Memory* (Mouton, The Hague)

Fillenbaum, S. (1974): Or: Some uses. J. Exp. Psychol. *103*, 913-921

Fillenbaum, S. (1975): If: Some uses. Psychol Res. *37*, 245-260

Fillenbaum, S. (1976): Inducements: On the phrasing and logic of conditional promises, threats, and warnings. Psychol. Res. *38*, 231-250

Flagg, P.W. (1976): Semantic integration in sentence memory? J. Verbal Learning Verbal Behav. *15*, 491-505

Flores d' Arcais, G.B. (1966): "On Handling Comparative Sentences". *Center for Cognitive Studies, Six Annual Report* (Harvard University Press, Cambridge)

Flores d' Arcais, G.B. (1970): "Linguistic Structure and Focus of Comparison in Processing of Comparative Sentences, in *Advances in Psycholinguistics*, ed. by G.B. Flores d' Arcais, W.J.M. Levelt (North-Holland Publishing Co., Amsterdam)

Flores d' Arcais, G.B. (1974a): Is there a memory for sentences? Acta Psychol. *38*, 33-58

Flores d' Arcais, G.B. (1974b): Semantic and perceptual factors in the processing of comparative sentences. Ital. J. Psychol. *1*, 267-302

Fodor, J.A. (1975): *The Language of Thought* (Harvester Press, New York)

Fodor, J.A., Bever, T.G., Garrett, M.F. (1974): *The Psychology of Language: An Introduction to Psycholinguistics and Generative Grammar* (McGraw-Hill, New York)

Forster, K.I., Dickinson, R.G. (1976): More on the language-as-fixed-effect fallacy: Monte Carlo estimates of error rates for F_1, F_2, F' and $min F'$. J. Verbal Learning Verbal Behav. *15*, 135-142

Franks, J.J., Bransford, J.D. (1972): The acquisition of abstract ideas. J. Verbal Learning Verbal Behav. *11*, 311-315

Fraser, B. (1971): 'An Analysis of "even" in English', in *Studies in Linguistic Semantics*, ed. by C.J. Fillmore, D.T. Langendoen (Holt, Rinehart & Winston, New York)

Frederiksen, C.H. (1975): Acquisition of semantic information from discourse: Effects of repeated exposures. J. Verbal Learning Verbal Behav. *14*, 158-169

Frege, G. (1892): Ueber Sinn und Bedeutung. [Translated in *Translations from the Philosophical Writing of Gottlob Frege*, ed. by P.T. Geach, M. Black, 1960 (Oxford)]

Frijda, N.H., Elshout, J.J. (1976): "Probleemoplossen en Denken", in *Handboek der Psychonomie*, ed. by J.A. Michon, E.G.J. Eijkman, L.F.W. de Klerk (Van Loghum Slaterus, Deventer)

158

Garrod, S., Trabasso, T. (1973): A dual-memory information processing interpretation of sentence comprehension. J. Verbal Learning Verbal Behav. *12*,
155-167

Geis, M.L., Zwicky, A.M. (1971): On invited inferences. Linguistic Inq. *2*,
561-566

Glucksberg, S., Trabasso, T., Wald, J. (1973): Linguistic structures and
mental operations. Cognitive Psychol. *5*, 338-370

Greeno, J.G., Simon, H.A. (1974): Processes for sequence production.
Psychol. Rev. *81*, 187-198

Grice, H.P. (1967): William James Lectures, Harvard University. Published in
part as "Logic and Conversation", in *Syntax and Semantics, Vol. 3: Speech
Acts*, ed. by P. Cole, J.L. Morgan, 1975 (Seminar Press, New York)

Griggs, R.A., Shea, S.L. (1977): Integrating verbal quantitative information
in linear orderings. Memory Cognition *5*, 287-291

Halliday, M.A.K. (1967): Notes on transitivity and theme in English: II.
J. Linguistics *3*, 199-244

Halliday, M.A.K. (1970): "Language Structure and Language Function", in
New Horizons in Linguistics, ed. by J. Lyons (Penguin Books, Harmondsworth)

Haviland, S.E., Clark, H.H. (1974): What's new? Acquiring new information
as a process in comprehension. J. Verbal Learning Verbal Behav. *13*,
512-521

Hill, S.A. (1961): "A Study of the Logical Abilities of Children". Doctoral
Dissertation, Stanford University

Horn, L.R. (1969): 'A Presuppositional Analysis of "only" and "even"', in
Papers from the Fifth Regional Meeting of the Chicago Linguistic Society,
ed. by R.J. Binnick, A. Davison, G.M. Green, J.L. Morgan (University of
Chicago)

Hornby, P.A. (1974): Surface structure and presupposition. J. Verbal Learning Verbal Behav. *13*, 530-538

Hunter, I.M.L. (1957): The solving of three-term series problems. Brit.
J. Psychol. *48*, 286-298

Huttenlocher, J. (1968): Constructing spatial images: A strategy in
reasoning. Psychol. Rev. *75*, 550-560

Huttenlocher, J., Higgins, E.T. (1971): Adjectives, comparatives, and
syllogisms. Psychol. Rev. *78*, 487-504

Huttenlocher, J., Higgins, E.T. (1972): On reasoning, congruence, and other
matters. Psychol. Rev. *79*, 420-427

Inhelder, B., Piaget, J. (1958): *The Growth of Logical Thinking from Child-
hood to Adolescence* (Basic Books, New York)

Johnson-Laird, P.N. (1972): The three-term series problem. Cognition *1*,
57-82

Johnson-Laird, P.N. (1974a): Experimental Psycholinguistics. Annu. Rev.
Psychol. *25*, 135-160

Johnson-Laird, P.N. (1974b): Memory for words. Nature *251*, 704-705

Johnson-Laird, P.N., Stevenson, R. (1970): Memory for syntacs. Nature *227*,
412-413

Johnson-Laird, P.N., Tagard, J. (1969): How implication is understood. Am.
J. Psychol. *82*, 367-373

Johnson-Laird, P.N., Wason, P.C. (1970): A theoretical anlaysis of insight
into a reasoning task. Cognitive Psychol. *1*, 134-148

Jones, S. (1970): Visual and verbal processes in problem solving. Cognitive Psychol. *1*, 201-214

Just, M.A., Carpenter, P.A. (1971): Comprehension of negation and quantification. J. Verbal Learning Verbal Behav. *10*, 244-253

Just, M.A., Clark, H.H. (1973): Drawing inferences from the presuppositions
and implications of affirmative and negative sentences. J. Verbal Learning Verbal Behav. *12*, 21-31

Keenan, E.L. (1971): "Two Kinds of Presuppositions in Natural Language", in *Studies in Linguistic Semantics*, ed. by C.J. Fillmore, D.T. Langendoen (Holt, Rinehart & Winston, New York)

Keenan, J.M., Kintsch, W. (1974): "The Identification of Explicitly and Implicitly Presented Information", in *The Representation of Meaning in Memory*, by W. Kintsch (Erlbaum, Hillsdale, N.J.)

King, D.R.W., Greeno, J.G. (1974): Invariance of inference times when information was presented in different linguistic formats. Memory Cognition *2*, 233-235

Kintsch, W. (1974): *The Representation of Meaning in Memory* (Erlbaum, Hillsdale, N.J.)

Kintsch, W. (1977): *Memory and Cognition* (Wiley, New York)

Kintsch, W., Monk, D. (1972): Storage of complex information in memory: Some implications of the speed with which inferences can be made. J. Exp. Psychol. *94*, 25-32

Külpe, O. (1912): *Ueber die moderne Psychologie des Denkens* (Scherl, Berlin)

Lakoff, G. (1972): "Linguistics and Natural Logic", in *Semantics of Natural Language*, ed. by D. Davidson, G. Harman (Reidel, Dordrecht)

Lakoff, R.T. (1971): "If's, And's, and But's About Conjunction", in *Studies in Linguistic Semantics*, ed. by C.J. Fillmore, D.T. Langendoen (Holt, Rinehart & Winston, New York)

Langendoen, D.T., Savin, H.B. (1971): "The Projection Problem for Presuppositions", in *Studies in Linguistic Semantics*, ed. by C.J. Fillmore, D.T. Langendoen (Holt, Rinehart & Winston, New York)

Legrenzi, P. (1970): "Relations Between Language and Reasoning About Deductive Rules", in *Advances in Psycholinguistics*, ed. by G.B. Flores d' Arcais, W.J.M. Levelt (North-Holland Publishing Co., Amsterdam)

Levelt, W.J.M. (1978): "A Survey of Studies in Sentence Perception: 1970-1976", in *Studies in the Perception of Language*, ed. by W.J.M. Levelt, G.B. Flores d' Arcais (Wiley, New York)

Levelt, W.J.M., Schreuder, R., Hoenkamp, E. (1978): "Structure and Use of Verbs of Motion", in *Recent Advances in the Psychology of Language*, ed. by R.N. Campbell, P.T. Smith (Plenum Press, New York)

Lyons, J. (1968): *Introduction to Theoretical Linguistics* (Cambridge University Press, Cambridge)

Marshall, J. (1969): "Psychological Aspects of Semantic Structure", in *Encyclopaedia of Linguistics, Information and Control*, ed. by A.R. Meetham (Pergamon Press, Oxford)

Matalon, B. (1962): "Etude Génétique de l'Implication", in *Etudes d'Epistémologie Génétique XVI. Implication, Formalisation et Logique Naturelle* (P.U.F., Paris)

McKoon, G., Keenan, J.M. (1974): "Response Latencies to Explicit and Implicit Statements as a Function of the Delay Between Reading and Test", in *The Representation of Meaning in Memory*, by W. Kintsch (Erlbaum, Hillsdale, N.J.)

Miller, G.A. (1969): A psychological method to investigate verbal concepts. J. Math. Psychol. *6*, 169-191

Moyer, R.S. (1973): Comparing objects in memory: Evidence suggesting an internal psychophysics. Perception Psychophysics *13*, 180-184

Naess, A. (1962): "L' Emploi de la Disjonction chez les Adolescents", in *Etudes d'Epistémologie Génétique XVI. Implication, Formalisation et logique Naturelle* (P.U.F., Paris)

Newell, A. Simon, H.A. (1972): *Human Problem Solving* (Prentice Hall, Englewood Cliffs, N.J.)

Nisbett, E., DeCamp Wilson, T. (1977): Telling more than we can know: Verbal reports on mental processes. Psychol. Rev. *84*, 231-259

Noordman, L.G.M. (1972): "On the interpretation of conditional sentences".
Heymans Bulletins HB-72-118, Groningen. Also in *Linguistics in the*
Netherlands 1972-1973, ed. by A Kraak, 1975 (Van Gorcum, Assen)

Noordman, L.G.M. (1978): "Foreground and Background Information in Reasoning",
in *Recent Advances in the Psychology of Language*, ed. by R.N. Campbell,
P.T. Smith (Plenum Press, New York)

Noordman-Vonk, W. (1979): *Retrieval from Semantic Memory* (Springer, Berlin,
Heidelberg, New York)

Noordman-Vonk, W., Noordman, L.G.M. (1974):"A retrieval model for comparing
word meanings". Heymans Bulletins HB-74-149, Groningen

Noordman-Vonk, W., Noordman, L.G.M. (1975): "Semantisch Geheugen: Het
Geheugen uit de Vergetelheid", in *Psychologie in 1975: Theorie en*
Praktijk van een Veranderende Wetenschap, ed. by H. Gosker e.a.
(Tjeenk Willink, Groningen)

Norman, D.A., Rumelhart, D.E. (1975): *Explorations in Cognition* (Freeman,
San Francisco, Cal.)

O'Brien, T.C., Shapiro, B.J. (1968): The development of logical thinking in
children. Am. Educ. Res. J. *5*, 531-542

O'Brien, T.C., Shapiro, B.J., Reali, N.C. (1971): "Logical Thinking,
Language and Context". Paper presented at the Annual Meeting of the
American Education Research Association, New York City

Olson, D.R., Filby, N. (1972): On the comprehension of active and passive
sentences. Cognitive Psychol. *3*, 361-381

Paivio, A. (1971): *Imagery and Verbal Processes* (Holt, Rinehart & Winston,
New York)

Paivio, A., Begg, I. (1974): Pictures and words in visual search. Memory
Cognition *2*, 515-521

Paris, S.G. (1975): *Propositional Logical Thinking and Comprehension of*
Language Connectives (Mouton, The Hague)

Peel, E.A. (1967): A method for investigating children's understanding of
certain logical connectives used in binary propositional thinking.
Brit. J. Math. Stat. Psychol. *20*, 81-92

Polich, J.M., Potts, G.R. (1977): Retrieval strategies for linear ordered
information. J. Exp. Psychol. [Hum. Learn.] *3*, 10-17

Potts, G.R. (1972): Information processing strategies used in the encoding
of linear orderings. J. Verbal Learning Verbal Behav. *11*, 727-740

Potts, G.R. (1974): Incorporating quantitative information into linear
ordering. Memory Cognition *2*, 533-538

Potts, G.R., Scholz, K.W. (1975): The internal representation of a three-
term series problem. J. Verbal Learning Verbal Behav. *14*, 439-452

Pylyshyn, Z.W. (1973): What the mind's eye tells the mind's brain: A critique of mental imagery. Psychol. Bull. *80*, 1-24

Quinton, G., Fellows, B.J. (1975): "Perceptual" strategies in the solving
of three-term series problems. Brit. J. Psychol. *66*, 69-78

Reichenbach, H. (1947): *Elements of Symbolic Logic* (Free Press, New York)

Reitman, J.S., Bower, G.H. (1973): Storage and later recognition of
exemplars of concepts. J. Verbal Learning Verbal Behav. *4*, 194-206

Roberge, J.J. (1970): A study of children's abilities to reason with basic
principles of deductive reasoning. Am. Educ. Res. J. *7*, 583-596

Roberge, J.J., Paulus, D.H. (1971): Developmental patterns for children's
class and conditional reasoning abilities. Dev. Psychol. *4*, 191-200

Romney, A.K., d'Andrade, R.G. (1964): "Cognitive Aspects of English Kin
Terms", in *Transcultural studies in cognition,* ed. by A.K. Romney,
R.G. d'Andrade. Am. Anthropol. *66* (3, Pt. 2), 146-170

Rumelhart, D.E., Lindsay, P.H., Norman, D.A. (1972): "A Process Model of
Long-Term Memory, in *Organization of Memory*, ed. by E. Tulving, W.
Donaldson (Academic Press, New York)

Sachs, J.S. (1967): Recognition memory for syntactic and semantic aspects of connected discourse. Percep. Psychophys. *2*, 437-442

Searle, J.R. (1976): A classification of illocutionary acts. Language Soc. *5*, 1-23

Selz, O. (1913): *Ueber die Gesetze des geordneten Denkverlaufs* (Spemann, Stuttgart)

Seuren, P.A.M. (1975): *Tussen Taal en Denken* (Oosthoek, Scheltema & Holkema, Utrecht)

Seymour, P.H.K. (1973): Semantic representation of shape names. Q. J. Exp. Psychol. *25*, 265-277

Seymour, P.H.K. (1974a): Pictorial coding of verbal descriptions. Q. J. Exp. Psychol. *26*, 39-51

Seymour, P.H.K. (1974b): Generation of a pictorial code. Memory Cognition *2*, 224-232

Shapiro, B.J., O'Brien, T.C. (1970): Logical thinking in children ages six through thirteen. Child. Dev. *41*, 823-829

Shaver, P., Pierson, L., Lang, S. (1975): Converging evidence for the functional significance of imagery in problem solving. Cognition *3*, 359-375

Sherman, M.A. (1976): Adjectival negation and the comprehension of multiply negated sentences. J. Verbal Learning Verbal Behav. *15*, 143-157

Simon, H.A., Newell, A. (1971): Human problem solving: The state of the theory in 1970. Am. Psychol. *26*, 145-159

Smith, E.E., (1978): "Theories of Semantic Memory", in *Handbook of Learning and Cognitive Processes*, Vol. 6, ed. by W.K. Estes (Erlbaum, Hillsdale, N.J.)

Smith, E.E., Shoben, E.J., Rips, L.J. (1974): Structure and processes in semantic memory: A featural model for semantic decisions. Psychol. Rev. *81*, 214-241

Sternberg, S. (1969): The discovery of processing stages: Extensions of Donders' method. Acta Psychol. *30*, 276-315

Stillings, N.A. (1975): Meaning rules and systems of inference for verbs of transfer and possession. J. Verbal Learning Verbal Behav. *14*, 453-470

Tanenhaus, M.K., Carroll, J.M., Bever, T.G. (1976): Sentence-picture verification models as theories of sentence comprehension: A critique of Carpenter and Just. Psychol. Rev. *83*, 310-317

Taplin, J.E. (1971): Reasoning with conditional sentences. J. Verbal Learning Verbal Behav. *10*, 219-225

Taplin, J.E., Staudenmayer, H. (1973): Interpretation of abstract conditional sentences in deductive reasoning. J. Verbal Learning Verbal Behav. *12*, 530-542

Taplin, J.E., Staudenmayer, H.,Taddonio, J.L. (1974): Developmental changes in conditional reasoning: Linguistic or logical? J. Exp. Child Psychol. *17*, 360-373

Trabasso, T. (1972): "Mental Operations in Language Comprehension", in *Language Comprehension and the Acquisition of Knowledge*, ed. by R.O. Freedle, J.B. Carroll (Winston, Washington, D.C.)

Trabasso, T., Riley, C.A. (1975): "On the Construction and Use of Re-presentations Involving Linear Order", in *Information Processing and Cognition: The Loyola Symposium*, ed. by R.L.Solso (Erlbaum, Hillsdale,N.J.)

Trabasso, T., Rollins, H., Shaughnessy, E. (1971): Storage and verification stages in processing concepts. Cognitive Psychol. *2*, 239-289

Van den Bos, K.P. (1974): "Visueel-Ruimtelijke Voorstelling, Taal en Logisch Denken. Doctoraal scriptie, Universiteit Groningen

Van Duyne, P.C. (1974): Realism and linguistic complexity. Brit. J. Psychol. *65*, 59-67

Van Hout, R., Tijshen, J. (1976): "Presuppositions in een Pragmatisch Perspectief". Doctoraal werkstuk, Universiteit Nijmegen

162

Wason, P.C. (1965): The contexts of plausible denial. J. Verbal Learning Verbal Behav. *4*, 7-11

Wason, P.C. (1966): "Reasoning", in *New Horizons in Psychology*, ed. by B.M. Foss (Penguin Books, Harmondsworth)

Wason, P.C. (1968): Reasoning about a rule. Q. J. Exp. Psychol. *20*, 273-281

Wason, P.C., Johnson-Laird, P.N. (1972): *Psychology of Reasoning: Structure and Content* (Batsford, London)

Wike, E.L., Church, J.D. (1976): Comments on Clark's "The language-as-fixed-effect fallacy". J. Verbal Learning Verbal Behav. *15*, 249-255

Winer, B.J. (1971): *Statistical Principles in Experimental Design* (McGraw-Hill, New York)

Young, R., Chase, W.G. (1971): "Additive Stages in the Comarison of Sentences and Pictures". Paper presented at the Midwestern Psychological Association Meetings, Chicago

Author Index

Garrett, M.F. 3
Garrod, S. 4,52
Geis, M.L. 82
Glucksberg, S. 3
Goodnow, J.J. 10
Greeno, J.G. 10,51
Grice, H.P. 82,114
Griggs, R.A. 14
Gysen, E. 123

Halliday, M.A.K. 114
Handel, S. 13-15,58
Haviland, S.E. 2,4,16,80,114,151
Henderson, E.N. 1
Henri, V. 1
Higgins, E.T. 11-13,15
Hill, S.A. 68
Hoenkamp, E. 3,123
Horn, L.R. 80,115
Hornby, P.A. 117
Hunter, I.M.L. 13,14,32,55
Huttenlocher, J. 4,11-16,18,19,26,
    32,53,58

Inhelder, B. 69

Johnson, M.K. 3,4
Johnson-Laird, P.N. 9,13,15,18,19,
    21,71,73,78,110
Jones, S. 13,15,55
Just, M.A. 2-4,11,107

Keenan, E.L. 115
Keenan, J.M. 52
Keith Smith, J.E. 5
Keppel, G. 5
King, D.R.W. 51
Kintsch, W. 2,9,51,52
Külpe, O. 11

Lakoff, G. 115,128
Lakoff, R.T. 72
Lang, S. 12,13,21
Langendoen, D.T. 115
Legrenzi, P. 71,73
Levelt, W.J.M. 3,5,118,122,123
Lindsay, P.H. 9
Lingoes, J.C. 84
Lockhart, R.S. 9
Loftus, E.F. 66
London, M. 13-15,58
Lucy, P. 101
Lyons, J. 125

Marshall, J. 140
Matalon, B. 69-70
McKoon, G. 52
Meerum Terwogt, M. 73,79
Michotte, A. 3
Miller, G.A. 115,116,118
Monk, D. 51
Moyer, R.S. 11

Naess, A. 72
Newell, A. 10,11,31
Nisbett, E. 33
Noordman, L.G.M. 5,55,63,66,73,97,
    110,112,122
Noordman-Vonk, W. 4,5,66,97,110,134,
    138,144
Norman, D.A. 9

O'Brien, T.C. 68,69,71
Olson, D.R. 3

Paivio, A. 11
Paris, S.G. 69
Paulus, D.H. 68
Peel, E.A. 70

Subject Index

Inferential process 1-3,5,113,138,
147,148
Information processing approach 5,
65,67,147
Inspection time 23
Integration of information 1-4,8,
19,36,53,58,147
Intended meaning 3
Introspection 33,60
Invited inference 82

Kinship terms 6,113-146,150,153
Knowledge, integration with 1,2
factual 65,74,75,102,103,105,
107,108
of the world 2,4,6,96,147-150

Level of processing 9
Linear ordering 4,19
Linear syllogism 12
Linguistics 1
Linguistic theory, *see* Three-term
series problems

Male-female asymmetry, *see* Asymmetry
Marked adjectives, and unmarked 12,
13,19,26-28,39-41,44-47,49-51,
63,64,110,148,153
and contrastive sense 12,63,140
Marked-unmarked effect 27-29,34,39,
40,42,44-46,49,50,55,63,148
Material implication 68-72,76,78,
82,99
Maxim of quantity 82
Meaning component 122,123,130,131,
137-139,141,144,146,150,152,
153
Modus ponens 69
Modus tollens 69

Negation, and presupposition 113,
115,116,118,119,121,122,128,
129,139,150
Negative equative sentence 12-51,
147,148
New information 86,137
and given 4,5,114,115,117,152
and old 2-4,16,17,20,32,113-115,
129,147,149,152

Old information, and new 2-4,16,
17,20,32,113,114,129,147,149
152
Only if 72-95,149,152
Or 70-83,149
exclusive 70,72,73
inclusive 70,72,73

Perception, and sentence comprehension 3
Personal orientation 144,150,151,
153
Positive equivalence 78-80,99,153
Pragmatic factors, in communication
6,82,117,147,149,151,153
Presupposition 6,80,113-121,147,
153
and belief 115,117
and expectation 117,130
first order 128
higher order 116,127,128, *see*
also Background information
Principle of minimal negation 122,
123,150,152
Procedural semantics 3
Process model 30,37,96,103

Question, role of 23,31,35,41,59,
148,151

Reaction time 5
Reasoning process 1,7-62
  and semantic factors 34
  and syntactic factors 10,29,34,
    47,62,148
Recall, and comprehension 4
Recency effect 27,32,46,58,60,62
Reference point-subject effect 28,
    40,44,45,49,50
Representation, conceptual 9,66
  of conditional sentences 104,
    105,107,110,111,150,152
  of retrieved information 104-
    108,111,149,152
  of sentences 2
  syntactic 8,51
  wholistic 4, *see also* Coding
Reproduction, deficient 90
  meaning changing 90
  meaning preserving 88,90,91
Retrieval of negative information
    108,109
Rhem, and theme 114
Riddle 118,119,129,146,150
Rule of minimal contrast 123

Same sex effect 131,134,135,137,
    138,150
Semantic feature 124,127,128,144,
    see also Meaning Component
Semantic memory 4
Spatial paralogic theory, *see* Three-
    term series problems
Strategies in problem solving
  backward search 31
  focussing 10
  forward search 31
  progressive deepening 10

scanning 10
search-scan 11
Structural description of sentences
    2
Syllogistic reasoning 68
Symmetry, between male and female
    terms 125,136, *see also* Asym-
    metry

Theme, and rheme 114
Three-term series problems 12-64,
    147
  compressing strategy 13,27,32
  congruent items and incongruent
    13,19,20,27,32,49,50
  end-anchor 14
  end-anchoring effect 14
  homogeneous items and heteroge-
    neous 25-27,49
  image theory 14-22,32
  linear items and non linear 27
  linguistic theory 13-22,32
  new term 12,14,16,29,34,46,152
  pictorial problems 7,8,11,22,53,
    62-64,148
  principle of congruence 13,20
  principle of lexical marking 13
  principle of primacy of functi-
    onal relations 13
  provisional strategy 61
  pure placement task 15,16
  reference point as old informa-
    tion 13,16
  reference point-subject 16,27,
    28,40,44,49-51
  spatial paralogic theory 14,15
  unified representation 18,20

G. Herdan

The Advanced Theory of Language as Choice and Chance

1966. 30 figures. XVI, 459 pages
(Kommunikation und Kybernetik in
Einzeldarstellungen, Band 4)
ISBN 3-540-03584-2

Contents: Introduction. – Language as
Chance I – Statistical Linguistics. –
Language as Choice I – Stylostatistics. –
Language as Chance II – Optimal Systems
of Language Structure. – Language as
Choice II – Linguistic Duality. – Statistics
for the Language Seminary. – Author
Index. Subject Index.

G. Hammarström

Linguistic Units and Items

1976. 17 figures. IX, 131 pages
(Communication and Cybernetics,
Volume 9)
ISBN 3-540-07241-1

Contents: Introduction. – Spoken
Language. – Written Language. – Written
Language in Relation to Spoken Lang-
uage. – Spoken Language in Relation to
Written Language. – The Tasks of
Linguistics. – Bibliography. – Author
Index. – Subject Index.

Springer-Verlag
Berlin
Heidelberg
New York

H. Hörmann
Psycholinguistics
An Introduction to Research and Theory
Translated from the German edition by H.H. Stern
1971. 69 figures. XII, 377 pages
ISBN 3-540-05159-7

„...provides a comprehensive introduction to the psychology of language by concentrating on the behaviourist
conception...
the translation is written in a clear, concise and compact
English...
The substance of this book, which has become a standard
textbook in German as well as the brilliancy of its translation will certainly secure its position in the English
speaking world as well." *IRAL (Deutschland)*

B. Malmberg
Structural Linguistics and Human Communication
An Introduction into the Mechanism of Language and
the Methodology of Linguistics
Reprint of the 2nd revised edition 1967
1976. 88 figures. VIII, 213 pages
(Kommunikation und Kybernetik in Einzeldarstel-
lungen, Band 2)
ISBN 3-540-03888-4

Contents: Introduction. – Signs and Symbols. The
Linguistic Sign. – The Communic Process. – Preliminary
Expression Analysis. Acoustic and Physiological Variable
Information. – Segmentation. Forms of Expression.
Oppositions and Distinctions. – Paradigmatic Struc-
tures. – Redundancy and Relevancy. Levels of Abstrac-
tion. – The Distinctive Feature Concept. The Binary
Choice. – Syntagmatic Structures. Distribution and
Probability. – Content Analysis. – The Functions of
Language. – Perception and Linguistic Interpretation. –
Primitive Structures and Defective Language. –
Linguistic Change. – Bibliographical Notes. – Author
Index. – Subject Index.

Springer-Verlag
Berlin
Heidelberg
New York

"A general survey of modern structural linguistics by
B. Malmberg...
The book is essentially intended for the advanced
student, but others will also find it useful, since the author
manages to deal lucidly and intelligibly with a difficult
subject." *The Years Work in English Studies*